I Saw The Devil, I Saw God

By Charles Mwumvaneza
and Isaac Amirian

Cover illustration by Lindsey Denhof.

ISBN-10: 0615919014
ISBN-13: 978-0615919010

Wakesho Publishers/California

A Note From the Author

My goal in writing this account is not only to share my own experiences, but also to tell the "story of penetration"– the type of true story that reveals the deepest secrets of the human condition. Most of us will confidently declare our own goodness and purity of heart, but catastrophes like the Rwandan genocide paint a different portrait of human nature– an unsettling one. It takes the collaboration of millions of criminals, cowards, and opportunists to make such an historic failure of humanity possible. And when it hits, there are few heroes.

Caught in the very center of that bloody season, I learned unpleasant things about man, and in particular about myself; this is the sort of penetration that I am longing to share. I don't wish to inspire pity over my suffering, but rather to inspire a life lived by principle– incorruptible by intimidation or promises of selfish gain, even in the smallest matters. If only a few more of us lived thus, genocides would be impossible. Souls, and nations, cannot be bent to the will of tyrants when men and women fear only God.

Heaven forbid that any more of us should live through such a thing as the Rwandan genocide. But how often do we read about such things, or see them on television, and imagine that we would never stand by and allow such an injustice; that we would never watch our neighbors and friends handed over to killers or dragged away to prison without a trial? Yet when faced with even the smallest of our own tests of character, offered the smallest of prizes, we betray ourselves. We steal from our employers; we lie to our families; we fail to come to the defense of those hurt by gossip or bullying.

These pages of our story– the story of Rwanda– are my most precious gift to you, and the best that I have to offer. They tell the story of penetration. It will be up to you to decide how deeply. My prayer is that even in the times that

3

are the devil's hour of victory, we will be bold, seeing the face of God.

-Charles Mwumvaneza

Forward

My name is Charles Mwumvaneza. I am Rwandan. My country is a tiny but beautiful one, nestled in the Great Lakes region of sunny central Africa, not far from the equator. Bringing together 8 million people, Rwanda is known as "The Land of a Thousand Hills" for its rolling and fertile farmlands. I was born there in 1956, in a village called Gahini.

My father was a Christian pastor, and my childhood was a joyful and peaceful one, growing up with five brothers and two sisters. We played endlessly together in the grass, sang together in church, and studied diligently. We learned to read and write in Kinyarwanda, the national language, and in French. Always we were raised in an atmosphere of faith, learning about salvation through Christ, the love of God, and love for one's neighbor.

As children, we gathered together early in the mornings to pray, and to memorize the scriptures. Day after day my five brothers, two sisters and I attended to our spiritual disciplines– sometimes begrudgingly, sometimes fascinated by the exciting stories of the Bible.

It is often said that "God has no grandchildren," meaning no matter one's upbringing, no person is really a Christian until they make their own choice. It was when I was fourteen years old that my parents' faith finally became my own. I decided for myself that I would believe.

It's difficult to describe the peace and joy that filled my heart as I found myself living in the service of my new King! In the past I'd felt compelled to sing on Sundays at church; but now that I understood the true meaning of the old songs, I sang like never before! We formed choirs, held prayer vigils, and helped our missionary friends from abroad in their social work and evangelism. I can still vividly remember Mr. and Mrs. Peter Guilbaud from England, the Sizzler family, and the families of Cott, Harlding, and Jones,

5

among others. Alongside them, we helped organize school camps for education and ministry during the long summer vacations.

In Rwanda, as anywhere else, the transition from adolescence to adulthood can be difficult; filled with temptations and tests of character. I not only avoided those pitfalls, but thrived, and to that I attribute my faith in Christ, and the spiritual fire that burned within me.

As a young adult I studied commerce and accounting at the College Official de Kigali, then in 1982, at age 26, I found work at the National Bank of Rwanda, or BNR, in the capital city of Kigali. Over the course of nine years, I assisted the Department of Foreign Exchange as the exchange controller.

Here in the city I experienced a new level of financial freedom and stability. I married Jeanne Batamuliza in 1984, and our family grew to include three children: two boys, Yves and Luke, and a girl we named Lyndz, after my mother. We owned a large house in a pleasant neighborhood, and even employed household servants. Our lifestyle was far removed from the experience of growing up in the village– we were never in need of anything. Yet as our riches and responsibilities grew, I found myself neglecting the disciplines of my faith.

I was sinking into a typical, worldly life, concerned with material things and matters of business and personal satisfaction. Where in the past I had prayed fervently, every day, looking for opportunities to share the message of Christ and to help those who suffered, I now found myself consumed mainly with my own affairs. Looking back, it's extraordinary how easy it was to lose the true riches that had been mine all along.

Of course my new family and I never fully stopped attending worship services, praying, and practicing our faith.

But in many ways I found myself losing the Christ of my youth. Becoming poor. Even lost.

But my trust in an unseen, loving God would soon be tested even further– in ways that I could never have imagined.

I, my family, and my country were soon to pass through Hell itself.

The trouble began in 1990, when an ugly civil war overshadowed Rwanda.

The poisonous seeds of violence had actually been planted long before, by Europeans, throughout the past century. Belgians had colonized Rwanda decades ago, subjugating its people and dividing them into two classes, based on their wealth and physical features.

The "Tutsis" were what they called the favored ones– a privileged few through whom the Belgian government managed the poorer majority– the "Hutus".

Exalted above their brothers by the colonial rulers, the "Tutsi" came to be deeply resented by the poorer, oppressed "Hutu." At the behest of the colonists, they even whipped and subjugated the Hutu, who were mostly poor farmers.

Believing that they were efficiently overseeing the Rwandans by setting the few over the many, the Belgians, in actuality, had turned a united land against itself. They had created two opposing factions of Rwandans, where once there was a population indistinguishable by appearance, language, or culture.

The Belgians relinquished Rwanda back to her people in the 1960's, but the damage had been done, and was irreversible. In the newly independent state, the Hutu, bitter over years of oppression, now made life miserable for the Tutsi minority. Europeans had manufactured the racial and social distinctions between Rwandans; but the wounds and offenses inflicted during their colonial rule had been all too real. The foreigners had gone; the infighting and division continued. The Tutsi now felt marginalized and abused under the new government.

It was in 1990 that a rebel force of disenfranchised Tutsi invaded Rwanda outright, after 40 years of exile. They were the FPR, or Rwandan Patriotic Front. Open civil war had begun.

For the civilian Tutsis living in Rwanda, daily life quickly became all the more unpleasant. Members of the Hutu "tribe" were the ruling majority in Rwanda, and controlled the government. They accused thousands of ordinary Tutsis of treason and conspiracy with the rebels.

As for me, I cared nothing for the imaginary divisions between "Hutu" and "Tutsi." I am one of many Rwandans of mixed Hutu and Tutsi heritage, and members of both "tribes" had always blended freely in the villages of my childhood. Such classifications meant nothing to us. And although I cannot help but use those hated terms– Tutsi and Hutu– in the telling of this tale, let it be known that they are, and have always been, an offense to me!

That lack of prejudice wasn't enough to protect my livelihood in the year 1991. Neither was the fact that I was, officially and according to my identity card, catalogued as a Hutu. There was no hiding my mixed ancestry– I am tall, and bear some of the other features designated loosely as "Tutsi" traits. I was fired that year from the National Bank of Rwanda, without explanation.

Still not quite aware of the seriousness of the situation, and of the horrors that were soon to come, I put the ugliness of my prejudicial loss behind me, and found new work with a private company called *SOGEE* (Société Générale des Entreprises). I was the administrative and financial manager, and reported directly to the president and CEO, who became a dear friend. I never suspected that two years later he and his whole family would soon be dead, and that I myself would be only desperately clinging to life.

The infamous genocide against the Tutsi began on April 7th, 1994. It was committed with the government of the United States, the United Nations, and indeed the entire globe watching. Nearly a million men, women and children were slaughtered with an efficiency and speed that shocked the world. They were systematically killed, tortured, and raped; by way of the machete, the club, the grenade and the gun. Families were forced to watch one another die; churches and schools filled with survivors were set on fire. No grievance could ever justify such inhumanity.

What's more, nothing could explain the silence and indifference for which the international community is to be blamed. Among those dismissively commenting about the genocide, many have described it as if it were inevitable; a fact of Third World life. An acceptable loss.

By the grace of God, I myself would survive. But I would lose everything, and come repeatedly to the brink of death, because I was considered to be in league with the Tutsi rebels.

I would live on– only to then suffer for nearly three years in a military prison without a trial, because I was considered to be in league with the Hutu!

The genocide, and the years that followed, cost me my family, my marriage, my home, and precious friends. I was left in constant fear and danger of assassination. I suffered the rejection of my own people, in my own country.

I saw the Devil. And yet, I saw God.

In order to protect the safety and anonymity of the surviving people mentioned in this book, I have been careful, when necessary, to use fictitious names.

9

Dedication

To my dear children, and to victimized children everywhere.

To my beloved brothers, Guillaume and Benoit. To my cousin Ignace, his wife Gemina, and their children. To my cousin Viviane, and my dear nieces.

To my cousins Huss Kayonga and Kayitare, my dear Catherine, and her husband, an assassin's victim. To all of my lost friends and family– I will never forget your courage in the face of dying horribly, and innocently.

To the Biramvu family, especially Mrs. Verene Biramvu. To your son, Vianey, who refused to give us away when we took refuge in your house. I will never forget his bravery, and yours.
Because of us, Verene, your son lost his life. To your family I dedicate this story.

To my friend and dear brother Gaetan. Before the tragedy I thought you were just a friend, but you showed me another side of you– true love. You took an enormous risk by hiding and caring for a despised "cockroach", though I had never done anything meaningful for you to deserve your generosity. You are my brother and a true hero, and you will forever have a special place in my heart.

To all those who have been robbed of their childhoods, their educations, their futures, and their families.

To those who find the blessing of forgiveness to be a nearly impossible task.

To all of you, I dedicate this story.

Chapter 1
African Paradise

The Contracting Parties confirm that genocide, whether committed in time of peace or in time of war, is a crime under international law which they undertake to prevent and to punish.

In the present Convention, genocide means any of the following acts committed with intent to destroy, in whole or in part, a national, ethnical, racial or religious group, as such:

(a) Killing members of the group;
(b) Causing serious bodily or mental harm to members of the group;
(c) Deliberately inflicting on the group conditions of life calculated to bring about its physical destruction in whole or in part

Any contracting party may call upon the competent organs of the United Nations to take such action under the Charter of the United Nations as they consider appropriate for the prevention and suppression of acts of genocide...

-Convention on the Prevention and Punishment of the Crime of Genocide, adopted by the United Nations General Assembly, 1948

Kigali.

The CND building.

Another view of the CND.

That night was unlike any other night. I couldn't put my finger on the reason why.

The lightning outside the window had withdrawn; the thunder had briefly quieted down. Did it mean that a storm was coming? Even the sun had retreated quickly down below the horizon.

Our tiny paradise in the Central African Spring, endowed by the Eternal with its own particular, quiet beauty, was tonight unusually calm.

It has felt that way often since the children have gone. I sighed.

I was fond of our home. It was modern and comfortable, though not overly lavish. We were surrounded by congenial neighbors and friends, just beyond the bustle and noise of the city.

Inside our living room, the clock in the corner struck six.

We were going to miss meeting the *Afande*! I went outside into the warm air, greeted by the silence punctuated with the lone barking of a dog somewhere nearby.

I turned back inside, and paced back and forth within the house nervously. I felt as if there was something wrong in the house; something I was forgetting. I could not leave before remembering it. Perhaps something outside of the house? Soon it was 6:15. I would have to be going; my mind still unsettled.

My brother-in-law Kayimba, my cousin's husband, had asked me to take the two of them to meet an acquaintance of ours, an unusual man– the *Afande* Charles Kayonga, a military Commander of the *Rukaga* battalion.

Kayonga's troops weren't Rwandan government soldiers; they were *Inkotanyi* rebels, part of the FPR, the Rwandan Patriotic Front. These were members of a political party engaged in a civil war against the Rwandan Armed Forces. They were mainly "Tutsi" fighters, although some "Hutu" had joined them in their revolutionary cause.

After two years of bloodshed, the rebels had now marched into Kigali, Rwanda's political capital, to negotiate a cease-fire, with the United Nations acting as moderator. Protected by the U.N., the FPR was now headquartered at the National Development Council building in Kigali.

And that is where we were now going.

I dialed my brother-in-law's number; it rang several times. Just as I was about to hang up, his familiar voiced greeted me, sounding hesitant and fearful.

"Hello…is it Charles?"

"Yes, Kayimba, this is Charles, but you seem to be afraid. It sounds like you are shaking, *mon cher*."

"Oh yes. What can I say, with all these grenades and assassinations, no wonder! And my truck and the driver haven't returned yet. It's enough to make me shake, *mon cher*."

"Do you still want me to take you to meet Afande Kayonga?"

"Oh yes, of course!" he was emphatic, as if fearing a change of plan. "My wife still wants to come, too."

"No problem," I assured him, "as long as you are ready soon. If we arrive too late, he may not be able to see us. Follow us in your car to the CND building. Let's not take pointless risks by driving together."

I urged my wife Jeanne to hurry and get ready– we could not take the chance of arriving too late in the afternoon. Visiting Kayonga was not an easy thing to do these days, given his busy schedule. And today we would be stopping by unannounced.

For Rwanda's civilians, life was filled with talk of war and politics. We'd heard that after much deliberation between the government, the U.N., and the FPR rebels, peace might finally be at hand; the civil war over. Reluctantly, the ruling

17

Hutu regime had caved in to international pressure and agreed to offer the Development Council building as a shelter during the peace negotiations for the rebel FPR's military wing: the Rwandan Patriotic Army, or APR. The two warring parties had agreed to share in the rule of Rwanda.

The CND building was a modern and imposing structure among several others belonging to the National Parliament– ranked by the experts as one of the strongest structures in Kigali, second only to that of the Rwandan National Bank. Built on top of a hill, it was surrounded by three military bases, from which U.N. forces could secure and protect it, should the need arise.

The FPR army's presence in such a high-security building– right in the middle of the capital city, and among military camps belonging to the enemy– was beyond comprehension. Two years of relentless war waged by the FPR had left Rwanda's economy paralyzed, claimed the lives of thousands on both sides, and crippled the nation's infrastructure. Anyone suspected of collusion with the Tutsi rebels was subject to incarceration, torture, or execution. When the cease-fire was first announced, it was shocking to think that our government would allow the FPR's delegation to come and taunt them in their very center of power.

Charles Kayonga, whom we were on our way to visit, was the Chief Commander of this delegation from the Rwandan Patriotic Front. With him were the six-hundred "invader" soldiers of his own battalion, and other high-ranking FPR officials. Among the leaders they had left behind, in their Kinihira headquarters, were the politicians Colonel Biseruka and Mr. Pasteur Bizimungu– both Hutus.

Bizimungu had defected from the government to join with the rebels in 1989, following the assassination of his older brother by the regime of Rwanda's President, Habyarimana. His conversion to the FPR cause gave a new legitimacy to the rebellion, as now even some prominent Hutus were being inspired to join the rebel movement. The FPR's mission was becoming more than just a matter of tribe against tribe. Malcontented Hutus in the backcountry joined the FPR forces, which conquered large parts of the nation's Northern and Northeastern territory.

The rebels also occupied the Volcano region– and its famed national parks, to the dismay of wildlife and conservation advocates. *Le Parc des Volcans*, where both sides battled extensively, was home to the mountain gorilla, that rare and majestic species that is the pride of the entire Great Lakes Region of Africa. The gorillas, too, were shamelessly victimized by the violence.

The FPR, and specifically its military, the APR, attracted many defectors from the soldiers of the Rwandan army. In response, President Habyarimana's government cracked down ruthlessly against any possible traitors, with campaigns of intimidation and persecution. The rebels, in turn, used the crackdown to their advantage, creating propaganda to play upon the public's resentment and unrest, and committing violent acts of terror, which they blamed on the government.

"Let me brush my hair and powder my face, and then we'll leave," pleaded Jeanne, through the open bathroom door.

She seemed bravely oblivious to the danger hovering over Kigali, as she hurried out the door to the car, still giving last-minute instructions to the two beloved household servants in our employ. She looked, that night, the way I will always remember her: wide-eyed, colorfully dressed, both beautiful and kind. Her expression was forever eager; animated.

As we drove away, we looked back, as always, to wave goodbye to our two servants and friends, who were at the door to see us off. There was Higiro– the brilliant, strong, and outgoing young man who had grenade-proofed our living room and bedroom windows. He was taller than average, and muscular, with a dark complexion, thick lips hanging over a prominent chin, and jaws framing a wide face with a flattened nose. The very image of what was considered "Hutu."

A stark contrast to Yvette, possessed of all the physical traits associated with the Tutsi. And yet, she was Hutu on her father's side. As we disappeared from view, she and Higiro turned away and attended to their duties about the house, as faithfully as always; double locking and bolting the doors.

My cousin and her husband were waiting for us at the fork in our neighborhood's main road. They followed my Honda Quintet at a safe distance in their pickup along the ten-minute drive to the Development Council.

The FPR's grand entrance into Kigali had been a historic moment. The civil war had reached a stalemate, and the two sides had agreed to enter into peace negotiations. These talks resulted in a cease-fire, and in the signing of the Arusha Accords of 1993, which created a power-sharing government.

The United Nations Assistance Mission for Rwanda (UNAMIR), composed mainly of Belgian peacekeepers, had deployed ground and air forces along an area extending from Kigali all the way to Rwanda's border. They were there to mediate between the two parties.

White helicopters, emblazoned with the black United Nations logo, crisscrossed the sky, machine-gun ports open, ready in the event of an outbreak of violence. On the ground, a long caravan of oversized buses– a gift from the President of neighboring Uganda– comfortably carried contingents of the Inkotanyi rebels towards Kigali, surrounded by onlookers filled with enthusiasm, and fanaticism.

(The vision of the UNAMIR soldiers, armed to the teeth and ready to defend the peace, could not portend the cowardly indifference that would be shown by the International Community just months later, as violence tore Rwanda apart. When hundreds of thousands of defenseless women and children were systematically slaughtered, these same peacekeepers would choose their own safety. UN forces would quickly evacuate their own nationals and then flee the country, leaving the genocide's victims to their fate. "Leave Rwanda to the Rwandans" was a phrase that would often be overheard.)

Villagers lined up on both sides of the road as the Inkotanyi procession passed, jubilantly cheering, "Oye! Oye!" Some cursed the convoy in its steady progress towards Kigali, but for the most part the new order of shared power was welcomed with a spirit of celebration. As the caravan passed through the border town of Gatuna, it became a virtual parade. A group of motorcyclists were waiting there to burst into a synchronized sort of motorized dance, accompanied by the sounds of cheering voices, blaring horns, and roaring engines. Then they peacefully surrounded the convoy, to escort it the rest of the way to the city, surrounded by a sea of humanity dotted with waving FPR flags. Even the mayibobo– the poor street children who survived by begging and stealing– momentarily forgot their hunger, caught up in the hope for a better future that the procession represented. Asian shopkeepers emerged from their storefronts; students and their professors abandoned their classes to join in the welcome-party for the valiant rebels.

What a glorious moment of triumph for the FPR supporters, and what a harsh blow for the Rwandan government! Sympathy with the FPR had been repressed and stifled among the people, for fear of government reprisal. The sudden public show of support was shocking– and risky. The current regime was fuming over their loss of control. The Rwandan Central Intelligence Service was drawing up long lists of conspirators to be killed. Citizens gambled with their own lives by expressing any sympathy they might have with the Inkotanyi. And yet, they considered it an honor to speak with them or befriend them.

Through propagandist radio programming and other media, the ruling regime had painted the Tutsi *inyenzi*, or "cockroaches" of the FPR in the worst possible light. But the media campaigns merely fed the curiosity of some, by elevating the rebels to the status of near-mythical creatures. Many Rwandans had heard that the Inkotanyi soldiers had tails and other such fantastical attributes. The rumors only added to the rebels' mystique. There was an eagerness to learn more about them, and to see them in the flesh.

As for me, I was not politically-minded, but I sympathized personally with Colonel Charles Kayonga. I had known for months, from a friend exiled in Kenya, that this six-hundred-man battalion would be directed by him. I felt privileged to be his friend, as he was admired and spoken of everywhere, renowned for his fearlessness and that of his well-trained troops.

And accompanying him was the delegation's political leader, Kanyarengwe, former friend of President Habyarimana– now challenging him for the seat of power!

With the tense situation in the capital city, law and order were breaking down in the streets. Bloodshed was everywhere. A bomb had killed an entire family. A grenade tossed through the window of a home. A minister returning from a government council, shot. Homemade bombs exploding in the marketplace and on buses. The president of a radical Hutu movement, assassinated in broad daylight. The tensions in Kigali had become so dangerous that we had, some time ago, sent our children to stay with relatives in Kenya indefinitely.

We lived in constant fear. Kigalians buried their dead and mourned, night after tumultuous night. Something about our national character must have compelled so many of us to live on in the midst of danger, rather than flee the city. Where others might run, we remained, perhaps not knowing where to escape to, or why. We took courage in a naive hope that peace and stability were close at hand.

As for the very thought of a *genocide*– and the massacres of hundreds of thousands of innocents– we never suspected such a thing possible. All over the world the very idea of genocide, an attempt to eradicate an entire people from the face of the earth...it was the single most intolerable crime against humanity. In the wake of the Second World War, a newly-formed United Nations had decreed that any attempt at genocide would not be countenanced. They were bound by contract to come together to the aid of any people so victimized. In many respects, it was for this very reason that the United Nations even came into being. The U.N. itself was in force among us, keeping the peace. Despite the sporadic violence, surely we were, on the whole, safe...

With my brother Kayimba's truck following close behind, we were soon on the Kigali streets, brown and red with dust, and then under the lengthening shadow of the Development Council building.

As always on our visits to the commander, I stopped the car at the curb and walked towards the visitors' kiosk near the CND for a routine security check. We were treated with the extreme courtesy typical of the FPR rebels!

And when my car stubbornly refused to restart, we were amazed to witness the kind and disciplined Inkotanyi being ordered to help us push it all the way to the top of the steep hill enthroning their headquarters! There at the entrance to the CND was the usual long line of impatient people, waiting for authorization to get in. I couldn't resist feeling some pride at not having to stand among them.

After greetings, thanks, and an exchange of civilities (I was now on familiar terms with most of these brave soldiers) I announced, as customary, the reason for our visit. Jeanne and I had made the trip, with its attendant security protocols, several times since Kayonga and his mean had arrived in the city. But for my cousins, it was all quite intimidating.

One of the soldiers went to inform Kayonga about our arrival. As we were left waiting outside for a moment, Kayimba leaned towards me.

"Charles, are you sure that it's alright for us to put them through so much trouble for us?"

"Of course, do not worry. The Afande will be excited to meet you."

A few minutes later, the guard returned to inform us that the Colonel would only see my wife and me. Though I protested, he remained firm.

Kayimba and my cousin could hardly disguise their disappointment, as they had no choice but to turn back towards home. Jeanne and I sheepishly reassured them before they were escorted back to their truck.

"The Afande must be extra-busy today. We will stop by your place on the way home."

We followed the young guard inside, through several winding corridors, until we reached the private room reserved for Kayonga's trusted guests.

The soldier asked us to take a seat there; the room was unusually dark. Was it intentional? Had the bulb broken? We sat and waited in shadow.

Twenty minutes passed, with no sign of Afande Kayonga.

"Are you sure he is going to come?" I asked the soldier, who for some reason was still keeping us company. He did not answer, but instead asked us question after question. How did we know *Afande*? Where exactly did we live in Kigali? Were we born and raised in Rwanda, and what was our ethnicity? They were routine questions, meant to screen visitors, but we had grown used to not being subject to them, and found them a bit embarrassing. The guard also never missed an opportunity to bring up his own patriotism and bravery in battle.

Then the long-awaited Colonel finally arrived. He hugged us as usual, his gun briefly becoming visible within the jacket of his army combat uniform. He was dressed as if ready for action. And unlike at previous visits, this time his military escort did not leave the room, remaining at his leader's side. He was under orders.

We exchanged pleasantries, made small talk, inquired about one another's families. Despite all appearances, Kayonga was clearly impatient to leave. His frequent radio calls added to our discomfort. We spent only fifteen minutes with him, during which he excused himself several times to answer the radio. He also looked at his watch, suggestively. It was as if our familiar friend had transformed into someone else. I wanted to let him alone, but was unsure about how to politely break things off; we were relieved to finally hear him say that, regrettably, he had an urgent matter to attend to.

"Forgive me, friends, but the situation in the city has got us all quite busy at the moment. Please be sure to come again at a later time, and bring your brother and sister too, Jeanne. My men will escort you to your car."

We were confused and disappointed by Kayonga's demeanor, but our spirits lifted when we arrived back at our malfunctioning car. There we learned that the FPR solders were not only fierce fighters but also impromptu mechanics! In our absence they had inspected the ignition system, found the problem, replaced spark plugs, and filled the tank with gasoline!

Whether motivated by pure civility or by political gamesmanship, they had thoroughly impressed us. What's more, although we insisted, they refused any attempt at repayment of any kind! Our worries about Kayonga's ominous behavior were swept aside and forgotten by the time we were back on the road, grateful for our good fortune.

On the way home, we made a quick stop at my brother-in-law's home as promised, to tell him about what had happened. Minutes later, we were greeting Higiro and Yvette within our own walls, safe at home.

It was about 8:30 in the evening. Had we known that this was the last hour of peace and normalcy we would ever enjoy, we'd have surely savored it.

And then, the storm finally came.

Two sharp thunder-like booms, in rapid succession, seemed to come from everywhere. It was the loudest of any such noise, natural or unnatural, we had ever known. We jumped. There was no rain; no storm cloud.

All of our worst fears nagged at us as we ran to the doors and the windows, hoping for a sign of the source of the commotion. Perhaps criminals or terrorists had begun using mortar fire against civilians. Perhaps the cease-fire was already broken, and war had erupted in Kigali. The unusual conduct of commander Kayonga gave me grounds to believe the worst. For a minute or two we milled about in the front yard, each curiously guessing at what the sound might mean, and then nervously retreated indoors again.

In the safety of the house, the telephone rang. I answered. Jeanne's cousin Kigozi was calling from the city of Butare, more than 120 miles from us.

"Charles, are you well?"

"We are fine. Why?"

"Can you see the airport from where you are?"

"No. What happened?"

"The president's plane was shot down. Just as it was about to land!"

"What president?" I couldn't believe what I was hearing, nor process the implications.

"Kinani!"

26

It was the nickname of Rwanda's President, Habyarimana.

"Impossible!"

"It's true. You are going to be in grave danger. It's good that you had the presence of mind to get the children out of the country a long time ago..."

My mind raced in circles, anticipating what we might expect next– the retaliation, the rage that the Hutu loyalists would feel towards any and all Tutsis. The Inkotanyi would surely be blamed for the murder, whether rightly or wrongly. There might be riots in the streets. I turned to pass the telephone to my wife.

"It's Kigozi. She said President Habyarimana's plane has just been shot down."

"That's probably what the noises we heard were."

"We are lucky that we made it home in time," I stammered.

For five minutes, my wife listened excitedly as her cousin relayed the news. Her expression became one of joy and relief; as if the president's murder would somehow end oppression and war in Rwanda.

I was eager to regain the telephone. I had two sisters and five brothers, and couldn't shake the terrible thought of unrest or even violence erupting nationwide. Most especially, I worried about my brothers in the city of Kabeza: Guillaume and Benoit. Not only were they still living in the country, but their children were with them as well.

So lost was I in my nervous contemplation that I failed to notice that our friend and neighbor, Protogène, was standing in our doorway. I ran to greet him.

"Oh, Proto. How are you?" I hurried him down the hall and into the living room. "Forgive us, we didn't see you there. This news about an attack has frightened us. Come in."

"Is it true that the plane was shot down?" He seemed thrilled. "I do hope that this Kinani is dead. In any case, let's celebrate!"

I couldn't believe it! He had opened a bottle of beer. My wife joined us, glowing, and suggested to me that we bring out the champagne, to mark the occasion.

"Perhaps we should prepare to die, instead," I offered dryly.

Chapter 2
Pandora's Box

"I was shocked and deeply saddened to learn of the tragic deaths of President Juvenal Habyarimana of Rwanda and President Cyprien Nyaryamira of Burundi last night in a plane crash outside Kigali, Rwanda. The two Presidents were returning from a regional summit in Arusha, Tanzania, intended to bring an end to the civil wars that have plagued their two countries for more than three decades...

...I am equally horrified that elements of the Rwandan security forces have sought out and murdered Rwandan officials, including the Prime Minister, Agathe Uwilingiyimana.

I strongly condemn these actions and I call on all parties to cease any such actions immediately."

-Bill Clinton, President of the United States of America
April 7, 1994

The tribal names "Hutu" and "Tutsi" were in use in Rwanda as far back as the late 13th century. But all Rwandans have always shared largely the same land and society. They also speak the same mother tongue: *Kinyarwanda*. They lived together, shared villages, and intermarried. Hutu and Tutsi; the culture was a united one.

It was the arrival of the Belgians and other Europeans that led to the creation of the Hutu and Tutsi, as they are known today. After a brief occupation by Germany, the Belgians colonized Rwanda in the 1920's and stratified its people into separate social and economic classes. They chose those Rwandans with European-looking features (lighter skin, smaller noses, etc.) to be "Tutsis" and commanded them to subjugate the rest.

The Tutsis became the wealthiest of Rwandans (defined as anyone with ten or more cows); while the Hutu were the more humble farmers, and the Batwa pygmies were marginalized by all. The Belgians had their dealings mainly with those whom they had labeled Tutsi, and set them up as the superior class.

Please understand that the designations of "Hutu" and "Tutsi" are utterly meaningless apart from this history of exploitation! Those who benefit from, or subscribe to, this partitioning of the Rwandan people insist that there are stark physical, even genetic, differences. But to an unbiased observer, Hutu and Tutsi Rwandans are more or less indistinguishable, except by their identity cards, required since the colonial times to boldly declare either "Hutu" or "Tutsi."

The Belgians sponsored the continued dominance of the Tutsi at the expense of the Hutu until the 1960's, when they were forced to concede independence to Rwanda under majority Hutu rule. The chaotic transfer of power to the Hutu only served to add more fuel to the fire of hatred between Rwandans, all leading to the bloody dawn of April 7, 1994.

Our telephone rang again, and never stopped. Friend after friend called, asking about our safety, and for the latest news. One acquaintance of ours, who lived in view of the airport, thought that he could see a light there, perhaps a fire. But there was little else new to learn. News broadcasts repeated only that the president's plane had been shot down– no one knew by whom. I could reach none of my brothers by phone, and what news I gathered from friends and relatives was only the worst kind. President Habyarimana was beloved by Hutu extremists, and had been gradually arming and training his own personal citizen militia– the *Interahamwe*, throughout the country. There were going to be reprisals.

I slammed home the phone in frustration, and returned to the living room, finding Protogène and Jeanne still there. Their "celebration" had already begun.

"Proto, come to your senses."

"Boss,"– he was already feeling the effects of the alcohol– "the only thing that matters is to know that this Kinani is dead. We don't care about anything else."

"Maybe you don't. You are nothing but a drunkard."

He muttered that he'd become a drunk because Habyarimana hadn't given him a chance to work or go to school. But his casual outlook became a sober one quickly. We had kept the radio on for the latest news; now an official statement was coming from the Rwandan government. It harshly and unmistakably blamed the Tutsi rebels for the missile that had destroyed the President's plane, promising swift vengeance against the FPR and any Tutsis sympathizing with them. And if the government wasn't going to call for any patience or restraint, neither would the rest of the Hutu. We would have to act quickly to preserve our lives.

My first thought was to flee to the CND with Jeanne, for protection among the FPR forces there, but the word

31

everywhere was that the Rwandan Armed Forces and the Presidential Guards had already started catching people along Kigali's main roads– the areas around the CND in particular. A drive there would take us directly into danger.

It was possible that I could go on foot through the darkness undetected, along paths and between roads, reaching the CND by stealth...but then I had to consider my wife, who could handle neither a sprint through the bush nor the commandos likely to shoot us on sight. To leave her alone in the house would be a death sentence– mobs chanting "Hutu power!" would almost certainly arrive in our neighborhood soon, looking to indiscriminately avenge the man they called the Father of the Nation.

(I would later learn that those FPR supporters who did reach the CND that night were coldly turned away. I've often imagined what it would have been like for us to have shared their fate– sent back into certain death; consumed by hopelessness, stunned by the rejection of their own people, whom the day before had been their brothers until death or victory.)

New broadcasts on the radio came from the High Command of the Rwandese Armed Forces, reporting that the attack that had actually killed two Hutu Heads of State: Juvénal Habyarimana, President of Rwanda, and Cyprien Ntaryamira, President of the Republic of Burundi, along with other high-ranking figures accompanying them and ten crew members, including French pilots. This statement was repeated every twenty minutes.

(To this day, it has never been officially pronounced who is responsible for the assassination. The government blamed the FPR/APR for the attack, while the FPR accused Hutu extremists in the Rwandan Armed Forces.)

It was now past midnight. I was pacing through every room of the house, nervously looking for the ideal hiding place should we be met by a violent mob. I was surprised to find everyone else in deep sleep, as if unconcerned with the evening's incidents, and their meaning. Jeanne had retired to our bed; Protogène had collapsed onto a cot in one of the children's rooms.

For another hour I feverishly worked the telephone, hoping to reach my brothers and sisters, still with no success. I could no longer stand being the only soul still awake in an atmosphere of increasing dread. So I went from bedroom to bedroom, waking everyone up. I gathered them together in the living room: Jeanne, Proto, and the servants Yvette and Higiro.

I described the perilous situation as it was unfolding, until they shared my alarm. They listened– first curious, then concerned, and eventually afraid.

I reminded them of the recent assassination of Burundi's former President Melchior Ndadaye, and the violence that had followed. I begged them to consider that Habyarimana was democratically elected and adored by a mostly-Hutu population; that the racist ideologies feeding Rwanda's tensions were at a fever pitch. We were all familiar with the threats and hatred spewed towards the Tutsi daily on the radio in in the streets. We had to consider the near-certainty of rampages by certain Hutu militias, and the likely desire for revenge among the Hutus, many of whom had lost loved ones in the civil war and its related acts of terrorism.

We also discussed, in that nighttime council, whether there might also be some reason for optimism. There was, after all, at that very moment in Kigali the U.N. deterrent force known as UNAMIR. They were well armed and ready to intervene at any moment to keep peace in the capital. Besides, the FPR/APR forces would fight back if provoked, and the youth-movement political parties– the Democratic Movement of Rwanda and the Liberal Party–certainly wouldn't stand for any massacres of civilians. Such was our hope.

(Today, I realize with bitterness how mistaken we had been, on all fronts. The United Nations elected only to send a force to evacuate foreigners, and abandoned Rwanda, rather than risk any of their own troops. The FPR was unprepared for slaughter on such as scale, and overwhelmed. And members of the minor political parties even joined in the massacres.)

Then our conversation turned to another matter: even if we were not directly targeted, how would we survive without being able to freely go out for food or supplies? There were small local markets– who made outrageous profits in such situations– to which we might be able to risk a visit for groceries. We also had Higiro, our kind and fearless Hutu servant. He assured us that we had enough charcoal for the kitchen and that he would manage to find out where to buy a 100-pound bag of potatoes the next day.

The sun had still not yet begun to rise when we received another phone call– from my friend and employer, the CEO of *SOGEE,* concerned for our safety. He urged me to not leave the house, as the situation had become extremely serious. He wished us well.

Not long afterwards, he himself would be savagely murdered with machetes, together with his wife and brother-in-law.

It was beginning. From somewhere out in the darkness outside, we heard the first noises. We became deathly quiet, listening. There were gunshots. Shouting in the streets. "Protogène…" I could see him visibly shaking. "I think you had better spend the night here."

His earlier jubilation had now fully yielded to panic; there was no talk of celebration now. We could make out the distinct sounds of machine guns. Every minute they grew louder.

It's difficult to describe an outpouring of misery and suffering upon a nation so complete, and so horrifying, that it

34

can make a man doubt the existence of a just and loving God. It was just such a plague that was breaking out over our beautiful land at that very moment.

In the world of Greek myth, Pandora was a woman created by the gods and destined to bring misery to mankind. On her wedding day, she was given a jar containing all of the evils and misfortunes of humanity, and was forbidden to open it. Out of curiosity, she disobeyed the instruction given to her, and opened it, releasing a flood of evil upon the Earth. All that remained within the jar was Hope– and without hope, mankind could not bear the misfortunes which had come upon them.

From this myth, of course, arose the term "Pandora's Box," which represents the unleashing of a disaster.

For those of us caught up in the Rwandan horrors, the genocide is not a single tragedy, but an entire Pandora's Box of simultaneous horrors– enough to drive the last spark of hope and idealism from our hearts. I see the gods and fallen angels of hell emerging with their deception and seduction, covering all of Rwanda with a flood of miseries. Greed, corruption, prejudice, violence, betrayal, cruelty, poverty, injustice, and lust.

When hearts are broken by the blows of evil, and when there seems to be no sign of any remaining kindness or humanity in the world, then a soul glazes over. We run out of tears to shed, and only emptiness remains. That is Pandora. I know no better way to describe it. That night, as we wondered what might become of us in the aftermath of the President's assassination, we expected to face troubles. We did not realize that we would be facing Pandora instead.

When even in the aftermath of the genocide, many Rwandans still suffer; some in secret military prisons, even to this day– that is Pandora.

I must be frank and admit that I had never truly known what suffering is, before Pandora. Simply reading or hearing of such things, and attempting to compare them to my own greatest trials up to that point, was insufficient.

I had never understood the depths of human hypocrisy, but I learned them from Pandora's Box.

I had never before felt the pain of prejudice and discrimination, but I learned about it from Pandora.

I had always believed that greatness, wisdom, and intelligence go hand in hand with leadership and power. But Pandora taught me by experience that the most treacherous of men are often the most respected and admired.

I did not truly accept that many of the world's richest men could be so hungry for still more riches that they would not fear to dirty their hands with the blood of thousands, even millions. I couldn't believe it, until I learned it from Pandora.

I did not know that a man could lose his home, his family, and even his life, and that his cries for mercy could be looked upon by strangers not with pity, but with mockery and satisfaction. Pandora taught me.

She taught me the true depravity of men's hearts; the true depths of human sin. In all of our assumptions, we overrate ourselves. When we conform to society's reasonable expectations of us, we call it goodness. When we resist temptation only because we fear the consequences of giving in, we call it integrity. When we decry riches and opulence simply because they have never been offered to us, we call it austerity. And when we show kindness in order to win the praise and admiration of others, we call it love.

When Pandora came to Rwanda, the guise of human goodness fell away. Men were granted the right to kill– to take their neighbor's houses, wives and daughters, without consequence– and few resisted. As mortals so often rise and sink to the level of their leaders, so Rwandans eagerly submitted to the government-sponsored realization of their most secret desires, rather than the fear of God.

Because of Pandora, I have seen enough evil to make a skeptic conclude, as many have, that Goodness and Truth are only constructs– useful for controlling the masses, but abandoned whenever the usual order of things breaks down. And perhaps, for many, this is the reality. But I have also seen, in the anarchy of Rwanda, the mark of the Almighty upon His people. I saw incorruptible men and women who had discovered, in the grace of God, a prize more valuable than any on earth– even than life itself. It was a truth that I would soon come to learn, and because of it, I believe to this day, that the power of Christ is greater than even the worst suffering.

And we have all suffered…but very few have experienced Pandora.

Chapter 3
Keep Running

"I mention it only because there are a sizable number of Americans there, and it is a very tense situation. And I just want to assure the families of those who are there that we are doing everything we possibly can to be on top of the situation; to take all the appropriate steps to try to assure the safety of our citizens there."

-U.S. President Bill Clinton, April 8, 1994

Josias was our young Hutu ward, who had always been tremendously polite and helpful to us. After his father died in an automobile accident, his mother had asked us to take him in, as she could not afford to provide for him. He had lived in our home for more than eight years, and become a strong and hardworking young adult, devoted to our welfare, even now that he had a home and life of his own. Being Hutu, he did not fear the *Interahamwe*, oftentimes dealing with them in person. He was not subject to any of their restrictions.

At dawn that morning, Josias came across the lawn to meet us, lacking his distinctive grin and pleasant demeanor. He was traumatized; at a loss for words. We talked on the patio outside the living room. He had seen something that he could not describe.

All through the night and into the morning, the national radio station, RTLM, had been repeatedly calling on all Hutus to rise and defend themselves against their common enemy– theTutsi. The government had ordered civilians to remain at home, and be ready to give away the enemy wherever he might be found hiding. Our house was located at the junction of three roads.

Josias had watched the beginnings of the violence with his own eyes. He recounted it to us, as best he could. He had seen the young and the elderly, male and female, beaten to death. He had seen heads severed, and tossed into the streets. The Interahamwe possessed detailed lists; Tutsi individuals and families to be killed. They carried new machetes and automatic weapons. These were not disorganized mobs, spontaneously reacting to the President's death. It seemed to Josias that this killing spree had been planned for some time.

Josias' gruesome report was interrupted by the sounds of more shooting– the nearest and loudest yet. Interahamwe militiamen were setting up a base nearby. As instructed by the prefect of Kigali, citizens had begun to barricade all roads, so as to prevent the 'enemy' from fleeing to safety. We retreated back inside the house. There was no longer any thought that the danger might be exaggerated. I asked Josias if he could go back out through the rear door, and find out whether there was any safe escape-route we could take, perhaps to find asylum at the IAMSEA University (the African and Mauritian Institute of Statistics and Applied Economics). He was eager to see what might be done to get us to safety.

Three separate times he went walking, leaving us alone in the quiet, wincing at the sounds of the shooting outside. Each time he returned with little encouragement to give.

After the third outing, fear and gloom were written across his face. I pressed him for the truth he seemed reluctant to share.

"The Interahamwe," he groaned, "and the FAR, together. They are slaughtering Tutsis wherever they can find them, hunting them down inside their own homes. They are canvassing the neighborhood. It's really well-organized. It will only be a matter of time until they reach this house. I can't take you anywhere; they have control of everything…"

He then asked to take me aside privately, as if I had been keeping a great secret from my wife.

As soon as we were alone, he lowered his voice and looked me in the eye earnestly. "Is it true, Charles," he asked, his hands clasping both my shoulders, "that you are harboring *Inkotanyis* in your home?"

"No! Why?"

"They say that you have a hoard of weapons, and that you are gathering your own personal army, ready to fight the Interahamwe or the FAR!"

Josias knew us well; he needed little convincing that the rumor was absurd. His advice to me was that I go with him to the front gate to try and pacify the most fanatical Hutus neighbors nearby; perhaps by giving them bribe-

41

money. Many of them had been our friends, and if we could gain their trust, they might protect us. Josias was no longer the humble and eager ward I had known; he had gone from offering suggestions to giving orders. Our lives were in his hands.

Among those enraged against me, he mentioned names that were familiar. A neighbor by the name of Murokore. Claude, a native of Ruhengeri. It made sense to try and negotiate; to bring the gossip about me under control while there was still a chance. I had known them for years. Perhaps they'd be reasonable and persuade the militias to spare us. With Josias, I stepped outside.

As soon as I passed through the gate outside of our property, heading towards the main road, a volley of gunshots was fired at me from a distance. I spun around and sprinted back, not stopping or looking behind until I was safely indoors.

I ordered everyone to lock the doors and move to the center of the house. They had already started to ransack and pillage their way through Tutsi homes, killing Tutsis, anyone considered as such by the Interahamwe, and anyone in collusion with them, based on lists that the regime had been drawing up for some time. For whatever reason, I was prominent on those lists– considered a major threat.

My wife hysterically searched me for injuries, chiding me for going out into danger so foolishly. There was a good deal of confusion and shouting about what to do next. The brave Josias turned to unlock the door.

"It's no use, Charles. They've already started on your street. They have lists that the regime has been making for them– Tutsis to kill. You are a major threat to them."

"Why? Where did these rumors come from? They know we are not enemies."

"It doesn't matter. Someone wants your house and land, probably. So they say you are a rebel spy."

"Can you do anything to stop them?'

"I will try. Pray for me."

Moments later, he was gone.

Protogène was still with us, now nearly hysterical with fear. He and Jeanne, both full-blooded Tutsis, trusted and counted on me to guide them, asking me repeatedly what to do next. They suspected that I might be immune to the persecutions myself, since my identity papers indicated that my ethnicity, officially, was Hutu. Even apart from the accusations that I was conspiring with the FPR, it was clear that my official Hutu status was no protection. It hadn't saved me from losing my job years before.

I was pacing throughout the house, praying more sincerely than I had in many a year. As a teenager, and as a college student, how I had once prayed! I had been in the habit of passionately asking God for wisdom, for the passion and ability to serve others, even for my future wife. It must have been years since I had last seen that fervent, spiritual young man!

And so I prayed, this time because there was nothing else to try. There was no way to flee the house without running directly into the arms of the waiting Interahamwe; nowhere to hide. I was at a complete loss, and the others– Jeanne, Yvette, Protogène – all considered me their last hope.

There was some measure of guilt in bargaining with the Almighty like this, in a time of crisis, after I'd made Him an afterthought so often in recent years. *God will not help you. You only pray because your life is in danger, because you have no other choice...it's too late to beg for favors now...* I tried to ignore the reproachful thoughts swirling in the back of my mind, but they could not be denied. I continued to pace and pray.

I could be thankful to have taken at least some precautions, long before things came to this. Acting on intuition after the start of the war, we had already evacuated our children from the country. Had our entire family been at home, the situation would be beyond impossible. To have had to watch them die–! I couldn't bear to even think about it.

Jeanne seemed defeated. She had resigned to sit and wait for death to come. I needed to find some place to hide her, at least, before thinking of a solution for myself and the others. Then if I could not save my household, at least our children might have their mother.

I thought of our neighbor and friend across the street: Alphonse Biramvu, an elderly Hutu man with a remarkable sense of duty and service towards others. He was a doctor, a pillar of our community; he had even served as an adviser to the National Republican Movement for Democracy and Development, or MRND– the party in power. And as for his wife, Verene, she was a veritable saint, and a close friend of Jeanne. It seemed to me that no mob would dare barge into their home. If only Jeanne could hide with the Biramvus, she might be safe!

I made up my mind to do whatever could possibly be done to get her to Dr. Alphonse's house.

From one of the windows I could see across the road to his front door. Directly between us was now a newly-erected barricade, guarded by armed men wearing the brightly-patterned shirts of the Interahamwe. The most formidable problem would be getting Jeanne past that fearsome roadblock.

I hurried her into the bedroom, along with Yvette and Higiro.

"I want to send Jeanne to Dr. Biramvu and Verene. I don't think they would turn her away."

Higiro had seen the heartlessness of the Interahamwe in person. "You would have to go directly around the roadblock. She would not make it."

"But they are coming here! We only have a few minutes before it won't be safe anywhere. I think that Dr. Alphonse's place might be immune from the searches. What if Jeanne had a disguise?"

"We can try. If they really could not recognize her...and if I escort her myself, perhaps." The threw up his chin. "God help us..."

Higiro and Yvette ran to bring some pants, a t-shirt, and slippers. She was to look like a servant, a *boyesse*. Together we rehearsed how we might deliver her safely to the Biramvus. She dirtied some loincloths and wrapped them over her clothes and head, as farmers did. For a finishing touch, she was given a jerry-can to hold in one hand, and another to hold on top of her head. She would have to make it from our house through the gate without being seen, and then walk casually to Dr. Alphonse's house in her disguise, without arousing suspicion. Even if the disguise worked, we had no way of knowing if Alphonse and Verene would be willing to shelter her. There was no choice but to hope.

Everything was ready in only a matter of minutes. We prayed together, maybe for the last time, Jeanne's hand trembling in mine. There, in that moment, I sensed Christ– just as I had always remembered His presence in years past. He hadn't left me, after all.

Whatever was to happen, there was comfort in that.

As soon as the area seemed clear, I watched, heart racing, as my wife and the valiant Higiro dashed outside, circling our property to approach the barricade from beyond our house.

I couldn't bear to look, nor could I look away. *The men at the barricade will surely see Jeanne in her disguise, and Higiro. He may be Hutu, but what if they know that he is one of our household?* I began to fear that my plan had sent Jeanne to her death. Her costume would be seen for the obvious ploy that it was…

And then, from the opposite side of the road, came Josias.

With the same friendly manner for which he had always been known, he struck up a conversation with the Interahamwe at the barrier, leaning coolly on the tree-trunks that had been laid across the road. He had watched Higiro and my wife approaching, and come to distract them.

I watched the servant girl who was secretly my wife, escorted quickly to the Biramvu's door. I saw her knocking furiously. A moment later, she was received into the house, safe.

The fear and relief I was experiencing within, in equal measure while watching my Jeanne's brush with capture, were a stark contrast to the silence in the house. I was alone in the quiet with Yvette and Protogène, all of us wondering what to do next. A glance in the direction of the telephone, still operational, set my mind racing through the names and locations of our friends and acquaintances. Among them there surely must be someone I had not yet called upon; someone who could help us!

One name did come to mind: Major Corière, an officer of the French Legion.

I dialed the number of the Director of the French Fund for Economic Cooperation (CFCE). My wife worked for this French institution, at their offices in Kigali; and at their disposal were capable French soldiers.

Not long ago, while on a visit to my mother-in-law's house, Jeanne and I had been robbed at knifepoint by thieves. They had forced their way into the house, ordered us to lie face down in the dark, and by flashlight proceeded to rob us of all we had– money, bracelets, necklaces, watches, and purses. The next morning, Jeanne had told her employers about the incident. In response, the Director of the CFCE sent Major Corière, a French Legion officer stationed in Rwanda, charged with protecting Westerners. The Major came to our house to interview us about the robbery– and left us with his phone number.

The fact that my wife was a CFCE employee, that Major Corière was already familiar with my house, and that the CFCE had access to well-armed French peacekeepers were reasons enough to call this gentleman for help. So I dialed, hands trembling. When he immediately answered the phone, I felt an irrational surge of hope.

I introduced myself as Charles, husband of Jeanne Batamuriza.

"Mr. Director," I stammered, "We have an emergency situation. The French are in control of the Kigali airport, aren't they?"

"Yes, we are but–"

"Sir, we're at home, near the airport. We are surrounded by the Interahamwe militia. They are on their way to break in and kill us. I'm begging you– please help us. You know that my wife works for the CFCE. This next hour could be our last."

I continued on, not wanting to give him a chance to respond before I'd fully stated my case.

"I heard that the Legionnaires are already evacuating foreigners. Can you send someone to rescue us as well? We'll pay you. As much as you want…"

His answer was precise.

"Mr. Charles, I am sorry. We have just received strict orders not to do any such thing for the…for the native Rwandans. We cannot evacuate you. Neither can the Belgians. I wish you good luck." He hung up.

My heart fell, the last of my hope extinguished.

I resigned myself to death; I would sit quietly with Yvette and Proto and accept my fate along with them, whatever it was. With luck, Dr. Alphonse and his family could hide Jeanne until the violence was over. Someday the children might return to be with their mother. But I myself would never rejoin them. I sank to the floor, my back against the wall.

There were footsteps on the veranda outside. The front door opened. I wondered what form my death would take.

It was Doctor Alphonse's son, Mafene, who rushed in, his eyes darting in every direction, finally spotting me, slumped in resignation in my corner.

"Charles, run. They have just killed Chriso and his wife, and they say that you are next in line."

Brave young Mafene! A Hutu risking his own safety to warn a man already as good as dead!

As abruptly as he had arrived, he was gone. But his heroism and the tone of his warning lifted me to my feet.

There was a loud, percussive burst from outside. Machine guns were firing on the house. One of the bedroom windows shattered.

Protogène bolted up from the couch and stood frozen, alert, like a hunted rabbit. There was nothing else I could do to save him…to save Yvette. But if I could escape the house...bring our assailants to chase me...perhaps I could lead them away. Perhaps they would be satisfied to kill only me, leaving the others alone. It was a fool's hope.

Another deafening series of cracking noise came from just outside. The other window in the kitchen burst.

"I'm going to run, Proto." He shook his head in protest. He would not be following me.

I ran directly past him, and through the halls, bursting out noisily through the backdoor and into the sunlight, where Interahamwe were forcing open the locked front gate. Uniformed FAR soldiers were nearby, firing. They had started to hurl projectiles at close range against the face of the house.

I sprinted across the back yard, and through the banana plantation next door. My flight had been so sudden that they did not immediately even notice me. It wasn't until I'd nearly reached the road that I heard their cries to one another. I had been spotted just as they began their advance on the front door. They turned and gave chase, pausing to take aim and shoot at me as I fled.

What happened then, I have no doubt, was a true miracle– evidence of a God who, when it pleases him, snatches a soul from death, for some intended future purpose.

Several militiamen and soldiers were chasing me, pausing only to fire machine guns or to throw grenades. I heard their shouts; I could make out some of their words. I heard and felt the thunder of grenades. Yet no bullets, no fragments touched me.

I'd always been an excellent runner, but the way I ran at that moment was beyond anything I'd ever thought myself capable of. A voice within was pushing me onwards, giving wings to my feet, seeming to say, *keep running, keep running, keep running*...I hardly touched the ground.

I was sprinting towards an open road in town, lined with shops on either side. My first thought was to take refuge in one of them, but they were, for the most part, closed. Worse, some of those same shopkeepers would have been among those chasing me, or standing guard at the barricades. I veered left instead, onto another, narrower street, only to be faced with a cluster of colorfully dressed, armed *Interahamwe*. I was running directly towards them. They shouted to one another. Some shouldered their guns.

Another side street was immediately to my right– the only possible route left. Losing little speed, I swerved and took it, narrowly escaping their line of fire. The new group of locals joined with the first in pursuit of me. My chest was heaving; my mind raced for a place to hide, a scenario by which this manhunt could end, apart from my death at the hands of formerly congenial neighbors.

At the end of this short street, directly ahead, was the Café *Umutekano*– a spacious bar and restaurant; closed in the daytime. I determined that I would try to get inside. It was surrounded by a high wall, with its lowest point a six-foot high locked gate, made of flat iron. I would have to jump over the gate. Still streaking at full speed, I leaped. More accurately, I flew.

In what I can only describe as another miracle, I propelled myself over the gate with my hands, landing with both feet on the other side. I felt lifted– as if by the "wings of eagles" I had read of in Isaiah the Prophet's book in my youth.

The sensation of feeling guided by a steadier hand than mine, the perfect execution of that full-speed vault, when every split-second counted...I credit God Himself, and not mere luck, or any skill of my own.

I was now within the walled, open courtyard of the Café. I had only a few seconds to find a place to hide, or a way out.

The wall protecting the Café extended all the way around; the only gap was the gate over which I had come. There were also two doors across the patio: one leading into the home of the bar's owner, and the other the entrance to the restaurant itself.

I could throw myself at one of the doors, and hope that it isn't locked...

There was only a moment left. I could hear the footsteps of nearly a dozen men nearing the gate.

*No time to gamble on the doors...*My eyes fell instead upon one of several piles of cardboard boxes and garbage against the gate. Some of the boxes seemed large enough to hide me.

I scurried underneath one of the largest of them and crouched down. My hands reached out and swept some of the paper trash nearby over the top and sides of the box, then disappeared back inside, where I made myself as compact, and as quiet, as possible, just as I heard the gravelly *thump* of boots falling onto stone nearby.

The first of them had scaled the gate and landed inside. Others followed, and I heard and felt footsteps, searching the grounds.

I huddled cold with fear, curled into an uncomfortable ball, terrified that any part of my body might touch the sides of my hiding place, moving it ever slightly, revealing me. I wished that I could will myself to stop breathing completely, afraid that even the sound of my racing heart would betray me. I expected the box to be lifted away at any moment, exposing my humiliated, cowering frame to the light, and to death.

Such a shameful way to die. Perhaps better to throw off this box and surrender on my feet than to endure this helplessness... But the militia were mostly searching inside the bar now. Whether it had been unlocked, or whether they'd forced it open, I do not know.

Three rounds of an automatic rifle were fired into the air. I nearly jumped. They probably meant to frighten and dislodge me. I stiffened; as if someone unseen closed my mouth and covered my eyes. Two successive explosions from grenades nearly rattled me. I had lost my nerves, still irrationally ready to leap out and yield myself. Yet I remained completely silent, and motionless.

There were two more shots fired. Then, an authoritative voice from outside the gate. It was probably the commander of the FAR group. He harangued his soldiers, and especially the militiamen.

"Idiots! Do you really believe that this *Inyenzi* running like a gazelle is still here? By now he's far away. Get out of there and be at the gate in five minutes, or else."

There was more shouting back and forth, from inside and outside of the Café. Among the voices in the disarray I heard, "He won't last long," and "we'll get him sooner or later."

Then the same commanding and gruff voice could be heard again, having assembled most of them by the gate. His last words before they filed away filled me with an equal measure of relief and horror:

"We have to kill all the Tutsis in Kimironko before noon, and you are wasting your time chasing this fool! We'll go to the Adjutant at *Kumwufe*."

Kumwufe was another café and bar, owned by an officer of the FAR called Nsanzabaganwa. He was familiar to me, and his name would forever be an infamous one. It was he who was in charge of coordinating the killing of the Tutsis in our neighborhood of Kimironko. I would learn later that it was he who had personally shot and killed my neighbor and friend Chriso, and his Indian wife Shenaz.

The immediacy of the last twelve hours had kept my mind racing. The frantic efforts to save my own life, and those of our household, had steeled me, until now, against the emotional weight of what would come to be known as Rwanda's darkest hour. As I waited for the soldiers' footsteps to fade, still cowering, still hidden, frozen in fear for twenty minutes that seemed like twenty days, realization finally, slowly, began to wash over my thoughts.

Chriso, dead! Shenaz, not even Rwandan, killed for no other reason than the unlucky heritage of her husband! All of our Tutsi neighbors and friends, no doubt, dead!

Likewise, our Hutu loved ones, reduced to heartless killers! Or forced, like Josias, to watch our men, women and children die without any show of sympathy or protest, lest they share our fate! My heart broke for what had become of those Hutu, as much as for the Tutsi. How could it be possible?

How many peace-loving Rwandans (to whom the title "Hutu" or "Tutsi" was as inconsequential as the length of one's hair or the size of the feet!) were now being forced to kill; to surrender their friends and neighbors, or else to die! And how many Rwandans of mixed Tutsi-Hutu heritage, like myself, had already paid with their lives for their fore-bearers' lack of bigotry? It was nearly 2000 years since the apostle Paul pronounced that we all, from every nation, were of "one blood," created and loved equally by one God. Had there really been any progress since? Could it really be true, if there was no faith, no love in the earth?

And to me at the time, the most perplexing question of all: How could all of this be allowed to happen? With UNAMIR– a United Nations task force assembled specifically to keep the peace in Rwanda– right here in Kigali? Why did the Interahamwe kill in the streets with such impunity, and the army alongside them? Could the U.N. allow such a thing to take place right under their noses? Where were they? Surely, I thought, an attempt to slaughter all of Rwanda's Tutsis could not succeed. It was a guiding principle of the United Nations to never again allow a genocide to take place like that which had decimated the Jews of Europe a half-century ago. Of what use was a United Nations, if not to put a stop to atrocities such as this?

I could never have guessed then, back at the beginning of our troubles, just how blameworthy the UN and its member-nations were in turning a blind eye to these crimes of the Rwandan government. Killing weapons of all kinds had been pouring into Rwanda for years— from France, China, Egypt, and South Africa.

At that very moment, as I huddled in horror at the revelation of the FAR's plans, American diplomats in Rwanda were reporting back to Washington D.C. that the Hutu government was calling for the destruction of all of the nation's Tutsis from the face of the earth— the very definition of genocide. But the United States would not intervene, nor would they plead for anyone else to do so. To the contrary, the American State Department evacuated only other U.S. citizens, and then called for the removal of nearly all the U.N. troops in the country.

U.N. safe-havens packed with helpless refugees were abandoned by UNAMIR, their United Nations flags pulled down. Churches and schools, filled with unarmed men, women, and children, were allowed to be quickly overrun with militias hurling grenades and swinging machetes, often as the deserting UNAMIR forces were still in view, driving away. Only when the scale of the carnage was undeniable— weeks after the fact— did American officials even admit the use of the term "genocide" to describe the systematic murder of 800,000 Rwandans. A genocide, after all, calls for immediate action. Expensive, inconvenient action. On our behalf, no action would be taken.

I ventured a fearful glance out from underneath the box, and then slowly, carefully, extricated myself. The place was deserted. I seemed to be the only living presence amidst those providential boxes and piles of garbage. Beyond were only the four high walls, the iron gate, and ominous silence.

It was about 9:30 in the morning. Too bright, and too early. If it were night, I could try to climb back over the gate and make my way to Dr. Alphonse's house by stealth, rejoining Jeanne. If my ideas about the taboos of Habyarimana's government were correct, the doctor's home was off limits to mobs, soldiers, and looters. We could hide there, at least temporarily. Maybe long enough to ensure our safety.

If there was now full-scale war in Rwanda, perhaps the FPR would win. International forces would reestablish peace, if we could only survive long enough to see it...

Reaching Jeanne and the Biramvus in the daytime was a fantasy. There were barricades and armed guards all along the roads. Remaining where I was, hiding until nightfall, would be equally dangerous. At any moment the proprietors of the *Umutekano* would appear. The place was sure to be occupied by early afternoon, for one purpose or another.

How easy it is to jump into a hole, and how much harder to get out! Moments earlier I'd barreled through this gauntlet of soldiers in a panic, chased by men with machetes and guns, surviving by impossible good fortune. Now, there seemed to be no other choice but to retrace my steps, and throw myself back into the lion's claws!

I remembered what Josias had said to me earlier that morning: *I heard that you have a hoard of weapons, and that you are gathering your own personal army...*

For some reason, I was considered a dangerous element. This was surely the reason why the Interahamwe's volunteer killers hadn't dared to launch an attack against our home at first. They wrongly believed– perhaps because of our friendship with commander Kayonga– that I was willing and able to fight along with the FPR, and had my own cache of weapons.

Was it merely a gossip-campaign, meant to discredit me? A lie concocted so that my name could be added to their killing lists, and my property stolen? Or did they really believe it? I had no way of knowing, but it explained why FAR soldiers had been sent as back-up to the Interahamwe surrounding our house.

A new strategy occurred to me. Since they believed I was armed and deadly, I could take advantage of their fears and go on the offensive. The group guarding the barricade would be mostly made up of neighborhood Interahamwe militiamen. They were local rabble armed by the FAR, not professionally trained soldiers...

If I played the part of the mythic, private commando for the FPR and charged directly towards them, would they panic? Could I lose them in the initial confusion, and then get to the doctor's house unnoticed? It was the only card that I had left to play, and was sure to be the most reckless thing I had ever done.

Rather than give myself any time to second-guess the decision, I scrambled back over the gate and into the street. There were no longer any soldiers nearby– they would be at the *Kumwufe* bar by now, receiving orders from the Adjutant. It was critical that I delay being seen by the civilian militia for as long as possible. I was lucky that the streets were deserted, but behind any window in sight there might be someone watching, willing to raise the alarm against me. I tried to walk confidently enough to not arouse suspicion. My heart pounded more and more violently as I came to the end of the street, and out into the open.

I was within sight of the barricade now. There were over a dozen local militia scattered around it, and no soldiers. There was no mistaking the brazen patterns of the short-sleeved Interahamwe uniform.

Some of them were arguing among themselves, fighting over the spoils they had taken in the course of their morning's awful work. A few others were focused on some papers, unable to come to an agreement about the best strategy for killing the remainder of their intended victims. Another group was in the act of beating a poor Tutsi, hunted down from God knows where.

I walked steadily towards them. As the first of them looked in my direction, I broke into a run.

I pretended to be drawing a weapon from my pocket, with intent to fire. I'd also removed my jacket and was holding it as if it covered a second firearm. I fully expected them to be a bit startled, and not realize that my "attack" was only the last desperate ploy of a terrified, unarmed man. I thought that some of the more cowardly among them might even scatter, while the others gunned me down at once. Nothing prepared me for the unbelievable happening, yet again, to my benefit.

All of them ran for their lives! Some ducked into demolished, looted storefronts. Others retreated towards the *Kumwufe* bar, seeking refuge with Adjutant Nsanzabaganwe and the FAR.

I was amazed at my own success as I stormed through a completely deserted barricade!

I forked sharply to the left, hoping to outwit anyone who might be watching my flight. I wanted to give them the impression that I was running towards downtown Remera– a few kilometers away. By the time they regrouped to hunt for me, they would think me far off, when in fact I would be hiding in a house no more than a hundred feet away. I had simply run in a circle around the cover of Dr. Alphonse's banana plantation.

I risked a glance backwards in my deceptive circuit, seeing no one behind me. From another direction I heard the heartrending moans of a poor girl pinned to the ground by a group of Interahamwe some distance away. They were taking turns raping her. I was enraged; but running for my own life, I did not stop.

I took several more detours before reaching Alphonse's house. To give away my destination would be to forfeit not only my life, and Jeanne's, but those of the doctor and his family as well.

My greatest fear now was being seen crossing the lawn. Once it was clear that no one was left in view of the house, I swung myself over the wooden fence, dashed to the back door and knocked, furiously.

Two large dogs appeared around the corner of the house. I knocked more rapidly, fearing that they might bark.

Verene, the lady of the house, at last came to the door and opened it without a word. She primly and quietly turned and walked down the hall.

I followed her to the bedroom where my trembling wife was seated. She had believed me to be dead. There was little to say, and it was said in hushed tones; both of our experiences had already taught us to make ourselves as quiet and as inconspicuous as possible, like hunted animals.

Our tender reunion was interrupted– by the sounds of more shooting.

We feared the worst for a moment and dropped to the floor. But the noise, we realized, was coming from the direction of our own house. Peering through the curtains, we could see them.

They were shooting and lobbing grenades against the house as if there were an army holed up inside. For an hour, and then another, they rained fire on what had once been our home. My heart fell for Yvette, for Proto. And Higiro– was he inside? Would his Hutu heritage protect him, or was he condemned by his association with me?

Verene joined us in the bedroom, visibly shaking. Her fear filled us with guilt and shame for placing her family at such risk.

"Charles, are there really no FPR soldiers in your house?" she worked up the courage to ask. Her fear was so great that she had difficulty uttering a word. I began to worry, as she did, that once they had thoroughly searched our house they would turn their attention to the Biramvus.

"Absolutely not. There are only Higiro and Yvette, and our friend Protogène."

Could they have had the luck to find somewhere to hide? Had they had a chance to escape the house when the Hutu were chasing me? Proto and Higiro had the look of bona fide Tutsi; there was no chance that their lives would be spared, if they were caught.

Every few minutes we risked a look through the window at the house. Little changed. At any moment we expected them to come for us; to hear soldiers crashing through the doctor's door down the hall.

The afternoon came, and we were still alive.

Verene reentered the room. She had been crying, and was still choking back tears. She could only speak with great difficulty.

"Jeanne. Charles. We have to abandon the house. Alphonse and I, and the boys. There is a bus coming to evacuate us, and some of the other neighbors. It's going to take us to Cyangugu. It's safer there…" It was a town in her husband's native district.

"Would it be possible…could Jeanne and I come with you? Would they protect us?"

She sobbed. "Even if they tried to hide you, they could not pass a single checkpoint with a Tutsi on board. They search every vehicle, at every point. They would just catch you, and probably kill everyone else for protecting you. They really want to get all of the Tutsi…you can only stay here and try to hide…I'm so sorry…"

Our only recourse was to remain at the house by ourselves, and wait for whatever destiny God had for us.

Verene left us the keys, shook my hand to bid me farewell, and shared a long, sorrowful embrace with Jeanne, who had long been her dear friend. A vehicle horn sounded outside, and the voice of one of the Biramvu's sons was heard, calling. Moments later, we were completely alone.

I left a devastated Jeanne there in the bedroom, and cautiously went to inspect the house for the best possible hiding place. Any noise I made was drowned out by the shooting; I could even hear the shouts coming from the force still surrounding our home.

There in the hallway were the two guard-dogs, lazily spread out on their sides across the corridor, half-asleep. At the sight of me they turned and growled. The Biramvu home was supposed to be deserted now; if they barked or attacked, we might be exposed.

I crept towards them as slowly as possible, making petting gestures. I wanted to win them over, but one mistake could reveal our presence. I was within arm's reach, and they remained still, until at last I was able to calm them. I turned towards the kitchen to find them some food.

On the table was what remained of some chicken that had been served for dinner, left half-eaten in haste. The dogs came eagerly for this peace offering, wagging their tails. They would stay quiet– at least for now– but I regretted having to waste food that could have been ours.

We can't open the door now, under any circumstances, but eventually we're going to have to send these dogs outside. They might attract attention to the inside of the house... Until it was safe to let them out, we would have to keep them quiet and well-fed. I had a look inside the refrigerator and pantry. There was enough food in the house to last a week, but the electricity to the area was gone, and most of it would be spoiled long before then.

And we'll be fortunate to live long enough to have to worry about food...

The windows filled the kitchen with the orange of dusk. The shooting and general commotion outside had mostly subsided, emboldening us to take a long look towards our house from the bedroom window. Every enemy seemed to be gone. It was clear that the house had been ransacked and pillaged, but why had they fired on it so heavily and for so long? Why such determination to destroy it? What had become of Yvette, Higiro, and Protogène?

Evening came, and we were driven nearly mad by the silence, the darkness, and the helpless waiting. As far as we could see and hear, the neighborhood was deserted and calm, but from further in the distance were the constant reverberations of what seemed like a firefight; a war zone. It kept us always on edge. We didn't dare to hope that the mob had given up on catching us; that our hiding place would remain safe and the danger eventually pass.

We had scarcely rested at all the previous night, and now struggled to keep our eyelids from closing. In the same bedroom where we'd spent most of the day sitting in ruin, anticipating either capture or death, we now slowly and quietly removed the mattress from the bed, laying it on the floor. We had decided that we would sleep as best we could.

For two hours we lied holding one another in the dark, still wide awake, straining at every sound.
A vehicle was on the road. It parked beside the house.

Instead of noisy soldiers breaking the lock and forcing their way inside, we heard a single set of footsteps, and the sound of the door being unlocked and opened with care. A familiar voice whispered for us by name. It was our Deo Biramvu, one of Alphonse's four grown sons.

"Deo, it is really you?" The sight of a familiar face delighted us! "We thought that you went with the others to Cyangugu."

"I did follow them there, bringing our car," he joined us in the bedroom where we sat. "But I couldn't stand sitting and wondering what had happened to the two of you. I told the Interahamwe at the roadblocks that I was coming back to check on the house."

"We are safe, thanks to all of you. I can't imagine why they did not search this place at all, after destroying our own house so violently. What has been happening out there?"

Deo had seated himself on the bed frame, his head sunken into his chest. He was shaken, and sorrowful.

"My mother told you nothing?"

"Only that you were all leaving Kigali."

"Not all of us are there."

With some difficulty, he recounted all of that afternoon and night's events to us. As the tale unfolded, we would understand just how narrowly we had avoided death–and at what cost.

The Interahamwe had exhaustively searched and looted our house by midafternoon, though Deo knew nothing of the fate of our friends inside. As they argued about where to search for us next, Deo had been present among the rabble, along with two of his brothers: Mafene, who had boldly come to warn me moments before the attack on the house, and Vianey, the eldest of the four.

One of the militia in the crowd had said, "I thought I saw someone jumping over Dr. Biramvu's wall before. He's probably hiding in there."

"We'll go get him there now!"

"What are we waiting for?" There was general agreement, though they reminded one another that the doctor was a well-respected elder in the community, and I would need to be extracted with as little damage to the house as possible.

Deo and his brothers interjected. They protested loudly against any attack on their home. Vianey, the eldest son, complained the most vehemently.

"You have no right to barge in there! Our parents are old. You're going to cause the death of them. They aren't suspected of anything! That Tutsi is not in there!" Deo and Mafene concurred.

One of the militiamen had then immediately shouldered a Kalashnikov rifle, and shot Vianey Biramvu, from only a few feet away.

His brothers cried out and raced to where the brave man had fallen, frantically trying to stop the flow of blood. Harsh words were exchanged among the militia in the chaos, as they rebuked the shooter for his brashness. Rifts and fights developed within the terror squad between those of differing native regions and political parties.

One of them remembered that Vianey's fourth brother was in the Army, stationed nearby at the Kanombe Camp. Fearing retaliation from the FAR for the murder, the pack dispersed, each working their way clandestinely towards their homes and to various bars and meeting-places, hoping to lay low and avoid any repercussions over the incident. Left alone by my house were Deo, Mafene, and their wounded elder brother.

Vianey gave his last breath before ever reaching the Kanombe Military Hospital.

As the heavy-hearted Deo finished his story, we understood that his brother's life had been lost for our sake. We knew now why that evening had been such a calm one. Vianey's death had secured our temporary safety.

Deo had come to us by claiming that he needed to keep the house protected from possible looters or vandals. With great sadness he lamented that his fellow Hutus had become fanatical, hunting down their Tutsi neighbors in their homes, killing any who dared seek escape outside. Machetes stroked, heads were severed, children were killed indiscriminately and women rounded up to be enslaved, raped or shot. The government had been planning for exactly this opportunity. On plantations, in downtown streets, in every Tutsi home; blood was everywhere. Deo's head fell into his hands.

"The French, the Americans, the Belgians, the Italians..." he groaned. "They all evacuated their own nationals from the country. The Americans made sure that all of their citizens were carried out. No one is evacuating the Tutsi civilians, or any Rwandans. Not even the ones who work for the embassy. Everyone was left here to die."

I asked him if he had heard about any of the Tutsi families with whom we were friends.

He replied that they had all been killed.

Elsewhere in Kigali, war was raging. Shells and bombs were tearing the city to pieces. Scarcely a few a seconds of silence could go by, at most, in between the cracks of gunfire that we couldn't help but hear from our sanctuary. Deo told us that it was the FPR. They had reacted to the massacres by resuming their war against the Rwandan Armed Forces.

Deo stayed with us throughout the night. Privately, not wishing to upset my wife, he told me the fate of my cousin Viviane, who lived in Kanombe, the city to which young Deo had rushed his dying brother.

After receiving several gashes from the machete, she had begged the Interahamwe to shoot her instead, offering money in exchange for a mercifully quick death for herself and her children.

Her torturers took the money, but denied her request, instead taking pleasure in watching her and the children bleed to death on the side of the road. Only late in the afternoon, several hours later, did death finally end their suffering. Viviane! I hope to be together with you in the peace granted by our Lord– you, and all of our cousins, nieces and nephews, Kabibi, Matinale, Robert, Mushyushya, Jeanne, Mporanyi, Kwizera! Mwizerwa Ignace and Gemima, Kayonga Jean Huss! How could your persecutors understand what light they had coldly extinguished! Indeed, may our Heavenly Father forgive them, for they know not what they do.

The Interahamwe knew horrible ways to kill: breaking bones, severing Achilles' tendons, and leaving their incapacitated victims in a hole or by the roadside to suffer a slow, agonizing death. I hoped to myself that if Jeanne and I were found, we might at least be shot. *Perhaps we can make a show of being armed, and they might fire upon us in self-defense rather than torture us...*

I might not have long to wonder, I learned. Deo told me that the Interahamwe had sworn to find me, and would not sleep until they had killed me as they saw fit. I was important to them.

Another day came and went without incident. That second night, Deo had gone out, and we were left with only the dogs and the anticipation of death as companions. Lying with Jeanne on our mattress, I could feel her heart beating wildly. By agreeing to sleep in shifts, taking turns, we were only now able to find rest.

The FAR had strong suspicions that we were hiding here. How long until they came? What news Deo could give us about the war offered little hope that the FPR might overrun Kigali somehow, and liberate us. And yet, we couldn't dare to flee, and be killed in the streets. It was better to wait; to extend our hours upon earth for as long as possible.

The exhaustion of three days without rest overpowered my vigilance and fear. My eyes closed in sleep.

I began to dream. My mind wandered far, far away from the senseless war, from the affairs of Hutus and Tutsis and their politics. I was safe with my children, in Kenya. To at last see them again! They were so dear to me; I was so close to them! How are they? How tall have they become? What has become of them, especially our baby girl, Lyndz, who was only two years old when she was evacuated?

I was playing with them just as always before; teaching them karate. We had a new home together. We had escaped Rwanda with our lives. How?

64

I imagined Jeanne and I, hiding in the empty tank of a fueling truck that belonged to a rich businessman friend of ours, and making our way incognito through the Rwandese border to Uganda...

I was half-awake now, only half-dreaming. Would such an escape work?

I rubbed my eyes, scolding myself for dozing off. By the time I had shaken off the heaviness of sleep, my mind was grasping for ways to realize this dream.

I let Jeanne go on resting as the first light of dawn appeared. I was mentally combing over every detail of our escape. It was an absurd idea, but it was *something*, and therefore better than waiting to be killed.

If Deo returns today with good news...if the FPR are going to win Kigali...then we will take our chances waiting here until the Inkotanyi come to save us. We will tell them about Dr. Alphonse, Verene, and their sons. We can vouch for them to the FPR, protecting them against any reprisals from the Tutsi...But if Deo brings more bad news, then we will be ready with this new escape plan...

Was it possible to survive a journey inside of a fuel tank? Even if it were empty, would we die from gas fumes? Who would drive the truck for us?

A more immediate problem– how could we get to nearby Kabeza, where the trucks were stationed? Apart from the checkpoints, traveling through hostile territory by stealth would be difficult, especially for Jeanne. I thought she might need toiletries and other necessities; she had nothing, and our own house was now little more than timber and stone!

I was so intent on materializing my wild dream that I started rummaging around the bedroom looking for items for her– a comb, underwear. It gave me a bizarre comfort to know she might use them in her new adventure. I sat down next to my wife, who had just awakened. There was no point telling her that I was making plans for an escape from the city. Not yet.

Morning fully came, and no with sign of Deo. I was imagining what route might be the safest to Kabeza.

The new day was disturbingly uneventful in the neighborhood. We could hear gunshots and grenades, closer now than before. Occasionally, a truck or a Jeep would roar at full speed through the large avenue across from the house, paralyzing us. Each time one of them passed by, we exhaled as if we had been snatched out of the grave. A time or two I peeked through the window to see only deserted streets– not a soul in view. I wondered if the Interahamwe had exterminated all the Tutsis in Kimironko. Maybe they had moved on to other districts. Did I dare hope that even the security checkpoints out on the roads were deserted now? Without Deo, we had no hint of what was going on around us.

Both dogs were growling. I decided to wait for the evening to let them out.

Outside, it was a radiant, sunny day. We were suffocating in the heat, with all doors and windows closed.

On the afternoon of that third day, Deo appeared in our bedroom. He had slipped in silently through the backdoor. The three of us sat in silence together, neither Jeanne nor I daring to speak for fear of learning the worst. He took a deep breath, stood up from the bed, and stretched, looking for the right words. At last he turned to me, and invited me to follow him into the living room. Whatever he had to say, he didn't want it to be in my wife's presence.

"The fighting has been really intense, Charles. The FAR has run most of the rebels out of the city, I think. They will not be coming here."

The Interahamwe were victorious, he explained, and they had decided to be done with me. With great difficulty Deo concluded that if we were found in their house, his family would be considered traitors and killed. Therefore, we could no longer endanger them all with our presence. The death of his brother had been enough.

66

There was no other choice but to leave immediately. Our enemies suspected that we were hiding there, and were coming to get us in the morning.

Our children: Yves, Luke, and Lyndz, safe in exile in Kenya during the genocide.

Taken in 1984. Among them, I am the only survivor.

Chapter 4
The Drift

"The international community must give highest priority to full, orderly withdrawal of all UNAMIR personnel as soon as possible... We will oppose any effort at this time to preserve a UNAMIR presence in Rwanda... Our opposition to retaining a UNAMIR presence in Rwanda is firm."

-Warren Christopher, United States Secretary of State
April 15, 1994

We would have to leave. There was no mistaking the danger that we posed to the Biramvu family with every moment we remained. One martyr, Vianey, had already sacrificed his life for ours.

To where could we flee next, and how? I thought perhaps that the IAMSEA school– the African and Mauritian Institute of Statistics and Applied Economics– might serve as the next temporary destination for us. Its vast campus was only a short distance away, and might already have been looted and then abandoned. There would be plenty of potential hiding places there. Reaching the place, however– or even traveling outdoors at all– still seemed like an insurmountable problem.

Despite all of the suffering that we'd already brought upon poor Deo, he offered us one final favor– his own unfinished house, only 30 meters away.

"You can hide there while you plan what to do next. From here–" he pointed out the living room window, "–you can see the front doorway. I'll go outside and look around; to make sure no one is watching and there are no cars on the road. Then you must both walk straight ahead, as quickly as you can. God be with you."

Inside a roll of cloth, I had wrapped up the few items I'd gathered for Jeanne. Deo walked nonchalantly outside, as if inspecting his own property for damage. We watched him through the window until he beckoned to us, hurrying us out of doors.

Our once-familiar neighborhood was now unrecognizable. My own home was a pile of wreckage, its fence destroyed. Deo guided us through the darkness towards his nearly-finished house, now in the center of a wasteland.

We were fortunate; thick rain clouds gave us some cover from the moonlight. There were intermittent light showers falling, and the occasional strike of lightning, which helped us to see where we were going. The rumblings of thunder mingled with the distant sounds of mortar shells and grenades.

Deo bid us a heavy-hearted farewell, and we hurried the rest of the way towards his doorless threshold. I wondered if we would ever see him again in happier times, wherein we might repay his family, in some way, for their selfless love. They were the first ray of light we had seen in man! If this present darkness and outrage were the Accuser's case against all faith and truth, then Dr. Alphonse's noble Hutu family was the evidence to the contrary. They had saved us; not only our lives but our faltering spirits.

We seated ourselves on the floor of a drafty hallway that smelled like lumber and earth. Once again we were alone in total darkness. Deo's house had no windows or doors; we could easily be seen from outside. It was a fine place to hide in the evening, but would become deadly by daylight. Sooner rather than later, we would need to be far from here; somewhere safe from the militias coming to search for us. But we were too afraid to begin the journey.

My heart and mind wandered back to the wreckage of our own house, and to the souls inside, whom I had left to the mercy of fate. It was visible from where we hid– a sad, collapsed shell, filled with demolished memories.

We'd neither seen nor heard any sign that Yvette, Higiro, or Protogène had survived the assault by the Interahamwe. Now, my curiosity was rising. It was as if the wrecked house were calling for my attention.

What if I were to explore its ruins…what hope or horror might I discover? Is it possible that even one of them could still be hiding there, alive?

I whispered my intentions to Jeanne, who offered no objection. She seemed as eager as I was to learn something of our friends' fate.

So pushing away my fear, I ventured back outside, underneath the stars. I crossed the street and stepped over the flattened fence, choosing my steps carefully, creeping through the broken stone and glass surrounding our former home.

Rather than use our front doorway, I entered through the garage, where I found that our Honda Quintet had become a carcass riddled with bullet-holes. Even in the house's demolished state, I could recognize the way to the living room, and then the kitchen, and finally the doorway leading to the backyard, through which I had fled from the initial assault by the militia, hoping against hope to draw away their fire.

There was no sign of life anywhere in the house– or of death.

I had steeled my soul, expecting to find, at the very least, the bloodstains of our loved ones. There was nothing. It was a mystery; I didn't dare to hope that all three of them had survived, nor did I want to consider what horrors might have befallen them if they'd been captured alive, and taken away.

I exited through the backyard, hiding for a while in the shadows, at the outskirts of the banana plantation belonging to our neighbor, Gaetan. From here I had a commanding view of the area. Just beyond Gaetan's house sat dozens of small cottages, most of them belonging to displaced survivors from northern Rwanda.

These northerners were Hutus; during the civil war in 1990, when FPR forces entered the country through Uganda, the northern provinces of Byumba and Ruhegeri became battlegrounds. The FPR had attacked and massacred the Hutu in these regions, and those who managed to escape the bloodshed fled south, many of them to Kigali, making the arduous journey on foot. UNAMIR had organized a settlement for them, where thousands took shelter in small huts and plastic tents, taking whatever jobs in the region they could find.

Among these displaced northern Hutus, the hatred and resentment towards the Tutsi was beyond words. Many of them were among the mobs that were now hunting and killing us indiscriminately. For them, the genocide was an opportunity to show the rebels that they were equally capable of dealing out pain and death. They were driven mad by the dream of recovering the land, property, and dignity that they had lost. Anyone who so much as *looked* like a Tutsi became the enemy; by exterminating them, they might have Rwanda to themselves, and lay claim to any Tutsi's property as rightfully theirs.

Only a week ago, these same good, gentle neighbors would not have hesitated to ask for any kind of help from us! Whether transportation, the use of our phone, financial assistance– anything– we were glad to call them friends. Now they were armed and hunting me!

Their cottages were clumped together, and stretched out as far as I could see in the direction of the IAMSEA institution. Although most of those huts were probably still occupied– many by Interahamwe– we could hide in their shadows by night, perhaps, and work our way towards the school, flitting from house to house...

There was little chance of success, and the movement through those huts would have to be done with great care and effort. There was no way to even know whether the Institute was abandoned– it could very well be filled with enemies. Still, after weighing our few options carefully, the IAMSEA still seemed as good as any hope we had.

We would have to move quickly; every hour of darkness remaining was precious. I returned to Jeanne, and reported to her that there was nothing to be learned about the fate of Yvette, Higiro, and Proto. I carefully explained to her my plan; how we might reach the IAMSEA by crawling among our neighbor's cottages. I tried my hardest to hide my own fears that we were most likely crawling towards our own death. I exaggerated our chances, suggesting that if the school were abandoned, we might hide comfortably there. Perhaps soon, peace would be restored.

Jeanne firmly refused. She was too frightened to even move from where she was. She preferred to wait for death to come, rather than race towards danger. The fear had overtaken her body.

For several minutes I spoke encouragingly to her. "Darling, we have survived this far. We know that the Interahamwe are coming, probably first thing in the morning. This house will not hide us. We have to be somewhere safe. If we can just be very careful and not give up, we have a chance to see our children again!"

It seemed that she was turning over my words in her mind, but she remained unresponsive. I pressed on.

"We are going to leave now, together. Let's go."

I turned and stepped down onto the grass, and slowly walked away from the house, hoping that she would set aside her fears and follow.

I walked all the way across the street, but did not hear her footsteps behind me. My gamble hadn't paid off. *I will have to walk back now. She really is not coming. I'll just have to try again to convince her to leave. Why had she not come? Would she really let me walk away without her?*

I turned back and saw her outside the house, seated with her back against the wall; frozen in fear.

Then I saw the reason why.

The shapes of two figures on the road, walking directly towards me, from the direction of the nearby bars and kiosks in town.

It was too late to return back across the road to Jeanne without being seen. To the side of me was a pile of debris; I dove into the center of it and hid as best I could in the shadow of some boards and heaped-up garbage. I settled into this hiding place as quietly as I could, but not as quietly as I liked. I heard their footsteps coming in my direction.

This is the end. They've spotted me.

Keeping in the shadows, I could view around the side of the trash pile to get a glimpse of them. They were coming slowly, haltingly. These two were neither soldiers nor militia. It was a drunken man, being helped along the road by a woman. I didn't move; I scarcely even breathed. *They will surely pass between my wife and I along the road, not seeing either of us...*

Instead, they turned and deliberately walked towards me.

They must see me! Should I stand and attack? Even if I can somehow neutralize them, how could we stay undetected then? If I curl up on the ground and pretend to be asleep, will they consider me just a collapsed drunkard, and leave me alone?

Each of these thoughts flashed across my mind before I had time to choose any course of action. Thankfully, before I could move, I realized that this man, who could barely stand on his feet, was only looking for a place to relieve himself. They were directly in front of me; he was struggling to pull down his zipper, his hands shaking.

The woman supporting him motioned to help, but he angrily refused. The inevitable happened; he began to urinate on himself, while simultaneously insulting and cursing the poor woman. He began to threaten her, claiming that he would strangle her if she didn't obey him properly.

"Dirty Tutsi whore, filthy cockroach, we will get rid of all of you soon..."

He included a great deal of foul language that I leave out. I now understood that this unfortunate woman was a Tutsi being held against her will, probably coerced into continuous rape and perhaps forced marriage in exchange for her life.

For the first time in all my days, I felt a genuine urge to kill another human being. He was drunk, and helpless. I had the power to end his captive's torture...but leaving her alone in the street might not prove to be helpful. It could even worsen her situation. Tolerating this horrible drunkard was her only protection from the fate of Kigali's other Tutsis. I could not know which course would serve her better. Whether because of cowardice or wisdom or both, I remained motionless.

With great difficulty the man succeeded in properly urinating– directly onto the pile of trash that was my hiding place. I suffered patiently, not daring to move. Finally, they turned to lumber back down the street. As their footsteps faded and were lost among the distant noises of war and thunder, I raised myself and looked back towards Deo's house, where Jeanne could still be seen crouched beneath its shadows.

My wife's momentary hesitation to follow me had probably saved both of us. Another happy coincidence, or another miracle?

I waved to her, and she emerged from the darkness, covered in a head-wrap to protect against the rain.

She now bravely crossed the road and joined me, rejoicing that I was alive and unseen.

We retraced my steps through our own backyard and towards Gaetan's house. I admired her newfound energy and determination! I was moving silently like a snake in the grass, and she was keeping pace wonderfully. We reached the cypress trim, surrounded by barbed wire, which was part of the rear fence of our property. The darkness was pitch black, and by now rain was pouring. We endured scrapes on our arms and backs, crawling over the collapsed barbed wire.

On our hands and knees, we stopped to rest at Gaetan's banana plantation, taking care not to fall into either of the deep holes dug into the yard behind his house. The holes were for toilets, meant for outdoor restrooms, not yet built. Such facilities were popular among middle-class African families. Arriving at the edge of the house, I left Jeanne alone and went to see if the area beyond was safe.

The rain had come to an end abruptly as I looked over towards the hundreds of cottages standing between us and the IAMSEA.

A handful of people were coming out of their homes and walking in my direction. More followed. I backed slowly back towards the rear of Gaetan's house, rejoining Jeanne.

Gaetan's home had also been converted into a shop– the only store in the area that closed late, and where groceries and other necessities could be bought at a reasonable price. The rain had kept neighbors from stocking up on groceries; now they were in a hurry to buy from Gaetan before it rained once more.

We would have to wait patiently for at least an hour, until the crowd ceased their shopping. As we hid on the ground, leaning between the back of the house and the nearby banana trees, I thought about Gaetan, our Hutu neighbor.

He had always been a friendly face to us; a soft-spoken, peaceful, sociable man. We did not know him well, nor even his full name. But we had often patronized his small shop, and chatted with members of his family. In spite of his humble means, he was known as a man of faith and character.

I wondered if we should change our nearly suicidal plans. What if we begged Gaetan for his help instead? He might be the only person we could rely on to safely take us to hide at the IAMSEA. Better yet, perhaps he could help me realize my foolish dream of escaping Rwanda by fuel truck...

I shared my private thoughts in hushed tones to Jeanne. To my surprise, she accepted the suggestion.

"Better to put our trust in Gaetan than to go among those houses, where everybody wants us dead," she whispered. "He is a godly man, not one of these Interahamwe."

"Do you think he would refuse to help us? Or maybe even give us away?"

"Even if he won't help us, I don't think he would want to be responsible for our deaths. Maybe he would send us away, but he wouldn't tell anyone…"

Our decision was made, and our future life or death depended upon the character of the Hutu neighbor whom we hardly knew.

The shoppers had now all returned to their homes, and I saw Gaetan himself coming outside among the trees. He was there to relieve himself, as his new toilets were not yet built. He was only two meters away from where we sat in the shadows.

I was tempted to call out to him, but hesitated to do so out of doors. Instead, as he turned back towards the house, I followed quietly and closely behind. By the time he'd closed the door, I had already slipped inside with him.

The weary shopkeeper started at the sight of me, as if he were seeing a ghost. I blurted out a stream of apologies and entreaties for help, making every conciliatory gesture that I could.

"Gaetan, I'm sorry. Please, don't shout."

He lowered his voice. "Charles...you're still alive? Those guns firing never reached you...how were you able to escape? And your wife...is she dead? Is she still alive? Have you heard from her?"

He continued to assail me with questions, drawing me farther from the doorway. But I still feared for my own safety, standing, as I was, within a Hutu household. *Was he still the same man whose kindness had been spoken of everywhere? Had these last few days destroyed his conscience as well? Was he really concerned for Jeanne and me, or was he gathering information to pass on to the Interahamwe?*

Gaetan stopped questioning and looked me over, seeming to sense my worries. Without a word he gestured for me to follow him into the adjoining room.

There in the dark, seated in a chair against the wall, was a man, younger than I, trembling with fear. His facial features were those of an ethnic Tutsi.

"His name is Fidele", said Gaetan. "He is my brother."

Moments later, Gaetan and I were exchanging our stories of the past week, in hushed tones. No one knew that Fidele and Gaetan were brothers; the boy had been visiting from his native district of Cyangungu just as the violence began. Gaetan had suffered much and risked everything to keep him hidden and cared for. Young Fidele had the misfortune of possessing Tutsi features; if his presence were discovered in the house, Gaetan, his wife, and his children would likely all forfeit their lives.

I was taken by their courage, and my spirits lifted all the more when it seemed as if he would be willing to assist Jeanne and I as well.

I threw my caution aside and decided to place all of my trust in Gaetan, confessing to him that my wife was, in fact, hiding directly behind the house. He turned the lights out in the room, to disguise his movements, and whispered that he would bring her inside.

"Wait here. We often have uninvited guests, even late at night. I will bring Jeanne to you as carefully as possible."

I stopped him, just as he reached for the door.

"Gaetan, wait...my checkbook is somewhere back at my house...I will give you all I have if you can get us safely to the IAMSEA. We are hoping to hide there."

His expression went from one of confusion to something almost like a smile.

"I can see you really don't know what's been going on around here!" With that he vanished into the humid air.

As soon as he was gone I began to suffer doubts. Suppose I had just led both Jeanne and myself into a trap? He might be fetching the Interahamwe to come and kill us. I considered following him outside, but to do so would show that I did not trust him; he might then have second thoughts about helping us. At last I concluded that there was nothing to do but to commit everything into the hands of the Almighty…

Minutes later, he had returned and was rummaging around in the darkness, searching for a box of matches. When at last he lit the lamp that was hanging on the wall by a nail, I saw with great joy that Jeanne was standing in the corner, soaked by rain.

I wanted to question Gaetan about the rest of his household– where were his children, his wife, and the nephew who lived with them in the house? More importantly I wanted to know what he had meant by his cryptic comment about the IAMSEA campus.

He brought a towel for Jeanne to wrap herself in, and sat us both down in the corner. "Yesterday," he whispered earnestly, "the FAR and the Interahamwe came to the Institute in force. There were hundreds of refugees inside. There had been a U.N. banner over the place. The peacekeepers were protecting the refugees. As long as they were there, the FAR would not risk attacking…"

He swallowed, his eyes turning downward. It pained him to labor through each word. "But the peacekeepers took their flag…they took it down. They drove away. They have left the country. No one was allowed to go with them, not even babies…only a few Europeans. Everyone else inside was left alone. Murdered…chopped to death. No one escaped. I heard wives…and children…begging for their lives."

He bit his lip. "It's not only at the IAMSEA. I'm telling you that UNAMIR is gone. I don't believe that there is any safe place left. The FPR have their weapons, at least. All of the rest of you are helpless."

"Impossible…" I was incredulous. Jeanne's mouth hung open as well. "Why could they not stay, Gaetan? How can they not understand that the Interahamwe will kill every Tutsi now? Even the children?"

80

"They have their orders." Gaetan had the look of a cynical and disillusioned soul. He had lost his faith in man.

"Not only the Belgians. The Americans, the French, the Italians. They all decided to leave Rwanda together. They would not risk one peacekeeper's safety for all the children in the country." He sighed. "So you cannot go to the Institute. The grounds were completely looted. Even today, they found a family still hiding there, dragged them out, and killed them. They have the run of the place now. It's out of the question."

Jeanne and I exchanged knowing and wondering looks. I turned to my new friend nearly in tears.

"Only minutes ago we were planning to pass by you and head straight to the Institute. Gaetan, an angel has certainly brought us here to your house! I really don't know why, but I see the hand of God looking after us everywhere. Gaetan, what shall we do now?" I feared that he would tell us that we'd have to manage on our own.

He explained that there was no house in which to hide us: the Interahamwe regularly searched through homes, and would surely find us and kill everyone. His house was also a shop– the most frequented in the neighborhood. Neither we, nor even his own brother Fidele, were safe inside the home.

My heart sank as I presumed that he was about to turn us away.

"There is a place I can put you," he continued, "...in one of the pits that we have been digging outside. They are for toilets, but the outhouses haven't been built yet. I was planning to hide Fidele there; you can go as well. They are very deep. Unless someone looks directly down inside, they won't see you."

He frowned and thought. A hole in the dirt wouldn't do for my wife. "As for Jeanne, I can talk to the Gasana family– we can trust them– maybe they can take her in and hide her while we consider what to do next. At least it might buy us a day or two."

Gasana was another Hutu neighbor whose name was well known to us. His wife was nicknamed "Maman Fils" and was loved by everyone in the community. They had asked us to be godparents for their child at his baptism, which we had joyfully accepted, happy to have a good friendship with Christian neighbors.

I quickly accepted Gaetan's proposal, though the idea of staying outdoors, in a hole in the ground, was an unpleasant one. We were desperate, and thankful.

As Gaetan left to meet with Gasana, I thought back to that first fearful evening in my own home, just after the President's assassination. I had frantically called every Tutsi friend and relative I could think of that day; anyone who might help us. How unexpected that our lives were now in the hands of two of our Hutu brothers!

Gaetan returned home after a long conversation with Gasana, to report that the risk of hiding Jeanne at Gasana's home was greater than he had thought. Their family's famous generosity and kindness meant that they were regularly suspected of sheltering the enemy. I, specifically, was being aggressively hunted for. At the risk of his life and that of his entire family, Gasana had nevertheless agreed to house Jeanne for one night.

With the evening at its blackest and quietest, Jeanne and I were forced to bid each other farewell once again. A second time I watched her walk away and wondered if I was seeing her alive for the last time. Both of us were wet, muddy, and exhausted. But despite our fear, there was a special peace in knowing that we were in the hands of caring friends. Even the specter of waking and sleeping indefinitely below the ground was not so repulsive to me. We convinced one another that we would meet again soon.

The narrow pit chosen for Fidele and I was remarkably deep– according to Gaetan, about seven or eight meters. The rain had subsided for a while, but was now beginning again, and we made ourselves ready to venture outside. Gaetan brought us enormous plastic bags for shelter, the kind used to package beans and grains. Such bags often served as makeshift umbrellas for shepherds and herdsmen.

Making doubly certain that the way was clear, Gaetan again put out the lamplight. At that moment his wife, Dianne, emerged from her bedroom for the first time. She had been nursing their infant son, and putting him to bed. Demurely she approached and shook my hand warmly, expressing her sympathy towards us for our misfortunes. I thought about the baby sleeping innocently in the next room, as his parents risked his life and theirs to protect us.

Gataen seemed to gain courage from his wife's equal determination to save our lives.

Young Fidele and I followed him outside in the rain, to the gaping pit. Over the past week I had seen workers climbing in and out of it by day, moving dirt. Now it was impossible to see the bottom. A surge of fear swept through me; I felt as if I were about to descend down into my own grave, or into hell itself.

There was no time to hesitate; every moment we stood outside, we risked the safety of our benefactor. Along the wall of the hole, near the surface, there were supports; I took hold of them and began the descent. In total darkness, I braced myself against the walls of the pit and scrambled down to the bottom, splashing down feet-first onto the watery bottom.

The fearful pit was also very narrow; by stretching out both arms I could place my palm against its opposite sides. Only by looking directly above could I make out anything other than total darkness, and that only a dim puddle of dark blue and indistinct black shapes, punctured by a faint few stars.

As quickly as it had come, my fear left me. I was determined to outlast my own government's reign of terror, however long it was, and by any means necessary.

I do not have to die. For my children, I must live.

By the time Gaetan's trembling brother joined me at the muddy floor of our new refuge, I felt completely at ease.

We stood together, motionless and silent, not daring to risk any conversation. The only sounds were from the booming of distant warfare, and the constant drum of raindrops tapping against banana leaves before splashing down into our pit, soaking us to the bone.

From time to time we'd wring out our clothes, doing our best to stay dry underneath our two large 100 kilo-bags. We were both shivering with cold; our feet completely submerged in slowly rising water. I could not see Fidele, but I heard his teeth begin to chatter as though he were suffering from a fever. The meager light of the moon and stars could not reach us; it was as though we'd been buried alive. I couldn't help but consider how helpless our hiding place made us as well. If someone so much as looked down into the pit in the daytime, we would be found, and have nowhere to run or hide. They could simply shovel mud into the hole and bury us alive...or more likely, toss a grenade in and be done with us.

I cannot bear to think this way. I would not simply let the Interahamwe kill me in this pit, without doing something to survive...

But every time I reenacted the scenario of being discovered in my mind...there was nothing to be done. We were truly helpless, and the more I considered it, the more unlikely it seemed that no one would think to look for us here. It was an obvious hiding place, a stone's throw from my own home.

I found myself praying silently; my last refuge. *God Almighty... I've lived a very selfish life. I let myself become lost; my heart was full of vanity and pride and looking for pleasure...I forgot about You. If I die here, I don't know whether I will ever see my children again...it's too late for me to live for you now. I can only trust in Your mercy.*
I slumped to the ground. *If you spare our lives and bring us out of here safely, I'll know that it really was only because of You. I will dedicate myself to you for the rest of my days...*

84

It felt as if a great weight had been lifted off of my shoulders.

I found myself thinking about Alexander Dumas' fantastic work of fiction, *The Count of Monte Cristo*. Its young protagonist, Edmond Dantes, had been trapped in an underground prison of his own, and attempted to escape by digging a tunnel out of his underground cell– using only a fork. He succeeded in his extraordinary escape, due to patience, ingenuity, and faith. The French would call such a remarkable feat "rocambolesque", after Rocambole, a character from old adventure novels. A fantastic escape or other such endeavor is still often called "rocambolesque."

Though *The Count of Monte Cristo* is only a romantic, fictional story, it became a source of inspiration to me. I decided that by the grace of God, I too, could achieve something downright *rocambolesque*. God had kept us alive to this point; I could feel His comforting presence. On my part, I must see what can be done to increase my chances, and do it well.

Unlike Edmond Dantes, I had no fork for digging. But in my jeans pocket I did have a small metal comb, made in China. I had taken it from Dr. Alphonse's house, while looking for personal items to bring along for Jeanne.

I will dig another hole going horizontally– a secret hole– that will hide us even if we are looked down upon from above. I was convinced.

Besides the comb, I discovered that I had another tool with me. My jeans were expensive designer ones, with two pockets on each side, connected by a metal plate. The metal could easily be removed, depending on whether you wanted to wear the stylish plates. Groping in the dark, I removed both metal knuckles. I felt for the sharpest part of the plates that I could use to accomplish my work. I quickly learned that it was more practical to dig horizontally, starting from one meter above the hole's bottom. This way, I could dig while kneeling in the mud.

I started to stab at that wall of dirt, underneath the pouring rain. My clothes and my body were soaking wet. The earth was soft and yielding, and the digging easy enough at first. I flung the clumps of dirt and mud on the ground at my feet and kicked and stamped them, Fidele all the while watching me curiously.

I paused and extended the second small metal plate towards him. If we could both dig, I believed, then by dawn we could have a tiny cave large enough to hold us both, where we might hide safely. My gesture seemed lost on him, so I whispered my intentions into his ear.

Fidele pushed my arm away and whispered back sharply, "That is madness! You are acting out of desperation. Better not to go through so much trouble, wearing yourself out. If we die, we die."

He had reached the point of despair. The survival instinct was no longer working. I went back to my work.

After another forty-five minutes, my makeshift tools had become too weak to continue tunneling with. The plates were bending every time I tried to dig. I found a way to use the metal comb for digging instead: by pulling out the tin rods from it and substituting my fragile, bent metal in its place. This arrangement worked fairly well for me, but the work was slow. My fingers were in awful pain; the metal was only about one millimeter thick, and at each stroke it dug into the skin of my palms and fingers. My arms were exhausted. My legs were weary from continually stamping the mud down and behind me as it tumbled to the ground.

After what must have been about four hours of digging, my mouth and my nose were filled with dust. My head and hair were covered with clay, and felt like a single clod of earth. I was pleased that my project seemed to be going well. The space I had dug was nearly large enough to accommodate me. It would be uncomfortable for me to squeeze inside, but most of my body would fit in. I redoubled my efforts.

A few more centimeters, only one or two more hours...at least don't quit working until dawn...if you double the size of this hole, it will be large enough to hide both of us during the day...one day I will return to this place and tell my story...people will be amazed and know that with God, nothing is impossible...
Such was my inner monologue, though it seemed insane. I was no longer thinking about threats from above, or anything else at all, other than digging. My body had spent its strength, and I was being driven from within, by the Spirit, by the Savior to whom I had entrusted my fate.

At the last moments of total darkness, just before dawn, I heard the sound of a human voice from outside the hole– a sound that dropped me to my knees in fear. My heart momentarily stopped; someone had crept up quietly to the edge of the pit. It was Gaetan, calling as loudly as he dared for Fidele. I exhaled in relief.
Fidele was sitting in several inches of muddy water, leaning against the pit's side where he had fallen into an uneasy sleep. Like me, he had started at the sound of his brother's voice. At Gaetan's instruction, Fidele scrambled back up to the surface.
Has Gaetan found a superior hiding place for us? I asked him whether I should come out as well.
"No, I am going to hide Fidele somewhere else."
With that lone terse statement, they were both gone.
I resumed digging.
And thinking.

I had never really firmly understood my identity. To this day, I'm still learning about my origins and ancestry. My father's line originated from the Hutu clan called *Ababanda,* and my mother from the Tutsi clan of *Abega.* This places me

87

among those Rwandans whose tribal "membership" is undefined– between two groups, Hutus and Tutsis, whose hatred for one another is unequaled. We "Hutsis" share a history and ancestry with both sides, but neither will claim us.

My mother and father had always refused to comment on the topic of ancestry. Ever since the occupation by the Belgians, the tension created between their two houses had been a constant trouble to both their families. So I questioned my paternal grandmother and uncle, and discovered the following.

I learned that I am a descendant of Mashira, a Hutu King. The neighboring Tutsi King, Mimbabwe the 1st, offered Mashira a marriage to his daughter, the princess Nyirantorwa. In return, Mashira offered his own daughter, Bwiza, to Mibambwe. This Bwiza, the Hutu princess, is legendary in our history as the most beautiful girl ever known among all the clans of Rwanda. Even today, songs and poems endure describing Bwiza as follows: *"Bwiza bwa Mashira budashira irora nirongorwa"*, which means "Bwiza of Mashira- whom everyone contemplates tirelessly, asking her hand in marriage."

Though this pair of marriages was politically motivated, it ignited the flame of love between Bwiza's father Mashira and his new bride, the Tutsi princess Nyirantorwa. Mashira stubbornly insisted on accepting the exchange of daughters offered by Mimbabwe, against the wishes of his closest advisors, who were skeptical of Mimbabwe's overtures of friendship. Indeed, behind the weddings was a sinister plot– after making a show of friendship between the two clans, Mimbabwe assassinated Mashira and his family. According to legend, the lovely Bwiza, now Mimbabwe's wife, committed suicide at the death of her father.

Besides being a vivid example of the types of stories told to stoke hatred between Hutu and Tutsi, this bit of oral history also explains the origin of a line of hybrid Hutu-Tutsi Rwandans, beginning with Mashira and Nyirantorwa, which has continued unbroken until the time of my own mother and father.

The town where I had spent most of my youth, Buganza, was never so deeply touched by the hatred between Hutu and Tutsi that infected the more politically-minded cities. "Hutus" and "Tutsis" were all Rwandan brothers there, as they had been for centuries before the European conquests. "Mixed" marriages like that of my parents were common where we grew up. But now, in Rwanda's darkest hour, hybrid families like mine were trapped in the very center of the horrors.

I dug continually, still thinking about my mother and father, as well as my children and the future that we could still enjoy together, if only we endured. I dug until the first light from the sun was visible. The rain had ended. I was finally able to dimly make out my handiwork. I had a damp, cold hole which I could curl up inside with some difficulty, but I found that after only a few minutes in this position, my body was cramping all over. If I heard someone coming, I would not be able to get into my new space quickly, and remaining hidden there for any length of time would be trying, and painful.

So I decided that before the sun fully rose, I would dig harder and make my hiding space wider and more easily accessible. I continued to dig. Slowly, deliberately. My aching muscles repeated the digging motion haltingly, slumped, my reserves of energy long spent.

It was only when the sunlight could at last penetrate down into our pit that I could clearly see the shape and depth of my newly-created hole.

It was amazing! A thing of beauty! Truly *rocambolesque*! With the aid of sunlight, I could see how it was possible to sit down on the ground inside the hole, with my legs facing towards the outside, and continue digging by expanding the space above my head.

I still wore a watch on my arm, completely covered with dried mud. I scraped at it until I could see that the time was ten minutes before seven o'clock. By eight o'clock, I had dug enough to be able to rest in a more manageable position inside the new hole, sitting or crouching with my side against the back of it. My shoulder, however, was still protruding out into the open air. I started to practice entering quickly into it and hiding my shoulder with the brown polyethylene bag. Covered in mud, the bag was nearly indistinguishable from the earth around it, and hid me, acting as a curtain over my tiny cave.

I was irrationally joyful at the experience of being able to easily enter my new "private apartment!" Completely spent, I returned to the my "living room" in the original pit, stretched myself freely, and collapsed against the wall, irrationally confident in my ability to at least do *something* defensive if threatened. As I sank into a deep, well-deserved slumber, I noticed that the blood on my two middle and ring fingers had run down both of my hands and arms, mingled with mud.

I started to dream about the Christmas Eves we would spend in my hometown each year, with my parents, and brothers, and sisters. All of us would leave Kigali and return to Buganza, in eastern Rwanda, to reunite with family. We each would bring a guitar and take turns playing and singing the spiritual Christmas songs of celebration, sitting around our decorated table, abundant with specially prepared foods.

I dreamt of the prayers and blessings we would share. There were my mother and father, brothers and sisters, my cousins, and elderly aunts and uncles! As evening came, we would sit around a bonfire, enjoying the cool breeze. I could hear frogs in nearby creeks, dogs barking at cows returning from their pasture. The songs of the shepherds and herdsmen, summoning their beasts home.

I dreamt of the traditional dances of Rwandese sisters, unique to the culture and legends of Rwanda. I had so many childhood memories of seeing their smiling faces, their pride in their ancient nation and customs!

For a precious few hours, there was no war, no constant fear, no hiding and crawling on our stomachs like animals. I was no longer collapsed in a mud-soaked hole, but unafraid, free, and contented.

My dreams were invaded by the sounds of shouts and screams. I was being hunted again. The flash of guns, the gleam of machetes. Men were hacking down bushes and brush. Someone was screaming orders to them: *Cut everything down! Dislodge the enemy!*

The dream ended. But above me, the hacking and shouting remained!

It was early in the afternoon. They had come, and were noisily chopping down Gaetan's banana plantation. Pulled suddenly from my fantasies, I remembered everything: the assassination, the persecutions of Tutsis and the attack on our house, our attempt to escape to the IAMSEA, and Fidele and myself hidden away underground. I nearly panicked as I leaped to my feet and saw that Fidele was gone, momentarily forgetting that he had been moved during the night.

The chopping noises and voices were all around me, and coming nearer. Muscles stiff and sore, I staggered into my horizontal bunker, squeezing myself inside. I could not help but make light splashing noises while doing so, to my horror. Once curled up inside, I reached for the plastic packing-bag, which sat nearby, soaked in mud. I pinned the edge between my shoulder and the roof of the tiny cave, positioning it as quietly as I could so as to cover as much of me as possible. It seemed horribly inadequate, now that my life depended upon it.

"Gaetan!" I recognized the voice shouting directly above me. It was one of my Hutu neighbors, Claude. "Gaetan, what are these holes for? You would not by any chance be a traitor, hiding one of these *inyenzi*?"

A second voice was heard, one I did not recognize. "These cockroaches are good at hiding. Better check inside the holes, check every corner."

A terrible few moments ensued during which I heard nothing. I didn't dare to breathe, fearing that the slightest rustle of the plastic bag would give me away.

Claude's voice echoed down into my hiding place. He was looking inside.

"I cannot see all the way to the bottom of this one. It's a bit dark."

"We'll bring a flashlight."

A third voice, also unfamiliar to me, joined the first two.

"Here's one. Check thoroughly."

I was as good as dead. Gaetan had moved his brother, and waited until daybreak to summon these killers. Perhaps he had not wanted to be directly responsible for my death. Perhaps he wanted to assure the murderers– for his brothers' sake– that he was not, as they called it, a traitor. Perhaps he had allayed their suspicions by telling them that he'd seen me near his backyard. Whatever the circumstances, I was, in my irrational paranoia and despair, certain that I had been betrayed. I braced myself, as best I could, for capture.

Yet another person whom I recognized by his speech was somewhere nearby, a man by the name of Lias. His voice was hoarser than I had ever heard it, most likely from days spent shouting orders to his Interahamwe teammates. He spoke authoritatively, and the others listened.

"The most urgent thing at the moment is to find Charles, wherever he is, and kill him. That is the top priority! I know there might still be some Tutsis in Kibagabaga, but we'll take care of it tomorrow. Keep looking for Charles!"

I have no need to tell you how this revelation chilled my blood. I had anticipated and thought about my own death for so long that I was ready now to embrace it as a sort of liberation. I had wrestled against it, struggled to cling to life, and now it had come to this. It was too much. My perspective widened; death, however unpleasant, would bring rest...and wherever and whenever it found Jeanne as well– if it hadn't already– we would be united again...

Claude maneuvered the flashlight's glow all around the base of my hiding place. He was standing directly above me now; right over the tiny cave that I had newly created, where I waited cramped and motionless. The light rested against the plastic bag, where my hand balanced it in place, then disappeared. He called out to his comrades.

"I checked the holes. They're both empty."

I had braced myself for the very worst, but not for this! Empty? While I am hunched inside? I truly believe that only God is capable of such a miracle! My heart and mind resurfaced from their morass and I was able to think clearly again.

I heard them advance upon the front to the house, where once more they interrogated Gaetan. Could they be certain that he was not protecting these Tutsi *inyenzi*? Poor Gaetan! He lied to them, denying having seen any Tutsis.

My eavesdropping on them gave me hope for Jeanne, too– the Interahamwe had said nothing of finding her, nor of Gaetan's poor brother Fidele. Wherever they were hidden, they must still be safe!

These killers were mostly *mayibobo*– local thugs and drunkards, augmented by a few laymen and military officials who coordinated their part in the genocide. I was certain that they had gone, as soon I could no longer hear their stomping and noise everywhere.

My legs by now were in terrible pain. I didn't dare leave my hiding place at first, though I allowed myself to stretch my limbs, one by one, outside of my tiny private apartment. Once again I could feel sensations in my arms and legs! The sunlight penetrated down into my hole more brightly thanks to the destruction of Gaetan's banana trees.

Leaves and branches were strewn about all around; I could distinctly make out the sound of a crow walking across them. If anyone were to walk towards me, I would know well in advance. With this assurance, I eagerly crawled out from the crevice that had saved my life, into the main pit.

It was 5 o'clock in the evening. I joyfully stretched myself, thanking God profusely for my good fortune. I was eager for nightfall, when I might risk a return to the surface to learn what had become of my wife, and whether the Interahamwe would return. I wondered whether Gaetan might be willing to help us get to the town of Kabeza, where we might put into action my scheme of fleeing Rwanda inside of a fuel truck…

Darkness overwhelmed me once again. I could no longer view my watch, and pondered when it might be safe to climb to the surface. My damp, dark hole had become beyond abhorrent to me– I felt that I could stand it no longer.

My inner conflict resolved itself late at night, when I heard Gaetan approach slowly, and call to me cautiously from above.

I scrambled up the slippery dirt walls with enthusiasm, longing to breathe fresh air. My skin was caked with dried mud; it compressed the skin of my face. There was no feeling in my head. I was torturing myself with mental images of a cleansing shower.

With some difficulty, I managed the feat of clambering back to the surface. Lit dimly by the moon, Gaetan's expression was one of shock and confusion. He hurried me back towards the house and through his door. Not bothering with any formalities, he asked me the question that was clearly weighing on his mind.

"You have returned here? Where were you hiding when the Interahamwe were looking for you in that hole, Charles? I thought that it was all over for you. I knew if they found you, they would accuse me of protecting you, and we'd all be killed for sure. These people don't show any mercy."

I interrupted him. "Where is Jeanne?"

"She is safe for the moment. Now Charles, when did you ever leave that hole? And where did you hide in the meantime? When did you go back to the hole?"

I couldn't sit down on his couch, covered as I was, head to foot, with dirt and mud. The shadow of Gaetan's eldest daughter appeared in front of me, as she brought a chair and motioned for me to take a seat. I reluctantly did so, dirtying it considerably. Gaetan continued to interrogate me in the darkness.

"Charles, I need to know, especially, where you were hiding. *Who* hid you? This is very important to me. I could approach that person and make sure that they do not betray us. I need to know if they will keep all of this a secret..."

He was both curious and frightened for his life. I promised him that I had never left the hole at all. I began to explain to him that I had dug a second hole perpendicular to the first one overnight, creating a cavity where I had hidden.

He disbelieved me at first. "Charles, are you mocking me? After all we have done to try to protect you, why would you not trust me? Tell the truth."

Finally I pulled from my pocket what remained of my metal comb. I handed it to him, my fingers still covered with hardened blood.

He turned it over in his hands. Relief washed over his face; he even smiled.

"Charles...this is truly *rocambolesque*."

A few minutes later, as the two of us discussed our options, Jeanne was escorted into the room to join me. Whatever her adventure had been over the last night and day, it had been harrowing.

I was desperately hoping not to be asked to return to the pit, facing infection and pneumonia, or being nearly helpless against any poisonous snake that might find its way inside. And the thought of being separated once again from Jeanne, with each of us risking our lives independently, was terrifying to us both.

My fingers were in terrible pain. They were swollen, still bleeding, and appeared to be infected. I felt some tingling all along both arms, and a slight fever all over my body. I was shivering from dampness and cold. I considered asking for something to eat, but refrained from looking for any additional favors from a family that was putting itself in jeopardy every hour for us. It was Jeanne, instead, who humbly asked whether I might be given some food. I was inwardly overjoyed as Gaetan's wife, Dianne, invited me to wash my hands– an offer traditionally made before inviting someone to come to the table.

She came with a jar of water, slowly pouring it over my swollen fingers. The heavenly aroma of well-seasoned meat filled the house. Soon Jeanne, I, Gaetan, and their three children were seated together in the traditional way, huddled on the floor together, legs folded underneath. I was served warm, steaming soup, and felt three days' worth of hunger dissipate, as if new life were spreading through my body.

It was simple fare, and it was the most wonderful food I had ever tasted.

While we were still feasting, our host resumed asking questions. How had I come up with the idea of digging a cavity, and how had I managed to dig with the comb?

"I cannot really explain," I said, between mouthfuls. "I came across the comb at Dr. Alphonse's, and put it into my pocket, thinking that my wife might need it. It turned out to have saved my life..." I paused. "If I had used a better tool, I could have dug much deeper. It turned out to be just enough." Merely talking about our brush with death sent a thrill through each of us at the table, as if God himself were surely in our midst.

Gaetan was turning an idea over in his mind. When he finally spoke, it was to say something that I did not expect.

"Charles, if you had a superior tool, could you continue digging tonight? Can you dig a hole big enough to hold you and Jeanne both?"

My first reaction was one of shock! How could this man think this way– especially believing that Jeanne could survive what I had just endured? Everything within me detested the idea of going back into that damp earthen grave! I protested. My wife, I explained, has allergies. She has serious sinus problems. Hiding her in a cold, moist hole would be disastrous. It would aggravate her condition. She would sneeze continuously. We would be heard from above and caught. My body had already been pushed to the limit; I might not be able to dig the tunnel twice as large as it currently was. And even if it were possible for us both to reside inside the hole over a long period of time, it was unlikely that we would go undiscovered before any kind of peace was reached. If the FAR completely defeated the Tutsi, we would never be able to escape! We could not live underground forever.

Gaetan dismissed my every protest with a sad shake of his head.

"It doesn't matter. I am sorry, but we don't have any choice, unless you want to take to the streets where the Interahamwe will kill you. Gasana cannot hide Jeanne any more– nearly every day they are searching his house. It's a miracle that we have kept her concealed until now.

"And I cannot take the chance of keeping you here. You know that my nephew, Modesto, lives in the annex attached to this house. What you do not know is that the young man has become a bloodthirsty killer. He frightens me. You remember him? You wouldn't recognize him now. He's gone mad!"

I was vaguely familiar with Modesto, the nephew. In happier times, I had seen him around Gaetan's shop. I wondered whether Gaetan had found it necessary to hide his own brother Fidele, from Modesto as well.

"If he learns that I have hidden you here," Gaetan went on, "I am sure he would not be ashamed to hand his own family into the hands of these raging Interahamwe. And as for your idea of escaping Rwanda in a truck– there is no safe way out of the city. Every road in Kigali is blocked. These people want to be certain that they have killed every Tutsi, and anyone who sympathizes with them. They're searching every vehicle. Please, Charles, I have thought about this. Stay hidden in the hole. I will continue to feed you from time to time, whenever I can."

My scheme of fleeing in a truck seemed foolish now even to me. I had clung to it, in my mind, hardly thinking it through reasonably until now. I could read the distress on my wife's face. She looked to me pleadingly– she was not happy with Gaetan's proposal. But his speech had disarmed me. It really seemed as if we had no other choice.

Our new plan was as follows: I was to return that night to the hole and dig all night long and through the next day. The following night, he would bring Jeanne. Attempting to keep Jeanne's presence in the house secret for a full day was a tremendous risk for Gaetan; anyone harboring the Tutsi "cockroaches" was sure to be killed, along with their family. If we were to be found inside the hole, however, Gaetan might at least have a chance at survival. He could try to convince the other Hutus that we had climbed in during the night, without his knowledge.

The rain had begun again, but now I welcomed it. The hardened dirt on my face and body could wash away now. I was going to descend once again into that miserable hole, and once again spend agonizing hours digging for my life, and for that of my wife as well. It was something to have decided on a course of action, at least.

Gaetan gave me a small hoe, one that had been used in the digging of the original toilet-hole. It was well-worn. I weighed it in my hand; it was far superior to a comb! For a third time I bid Jeanne goodbye. She was heartbroken. I smiled and jokingly assured her that I was preparing a new apartment for us, and that I would be receiving her there soon, just as it had been on our wedding day. Inwardly, I wrestled against the same despair.

Once again Gaetan and I stealthily crept across the yard under cover of darkness. Feelings of doubt and fear concerning Gaetan crept back into my mind. *Sending us both into this hole will make it easy for him to call the Interahamwe and tell them where we are hiding. No one would suspect him or his family then...*I drove the sinister thoughts away. *If he were going to betray us, he would have done it a long time ago. Besides, there really seems to be no other way. He has risked everything he has for us many times already...*
I descended back into my dreadful, familiar new lodgings. Gaetan waited above me to determine whether the sound of my hoe at work could be heard from the surface.

I hacked away at the soil inside my crevice for a moment before Gaetan whispered down to me sharply, "I can hear you. You will have to stop. The neighbors will ask about these noises."
"Find me something else then. Something sharp like a big screwdriver."
He disappeared and returned again waving something slender. I rose to the surface and took it– a piece of wood fashioned into a sharp spear at one end.
"This can help you, I think. Go and dig for a minute and I'll listen."
"It looks perfect," I slid back down and felt for the horizontal cavity I had dug. I began to dig into the soft earth

of its back wall. It was excellent– no noise. I motioned back to him that I was pleased with the tool.

And so I began to labor on my tiny tunnel once again. One new difficulty arose: the amount of dirt I had already displaced was collecting at the bottom of the hole, which had become noticeably shallower. I realized now why my first dig had taken as long as it had. The level of the hole was rising slowly, forcing me to raise the roof of my cavity in kind. As the dirt fell to the ground, I kicked it into the main hole and stomped it with my feet. Still, I was gradually rising, as well as digging the tiny cave deeper horizontally.

After six hours of grueling work, the pit had decreased from its original seven meters' depth to about five. I had expanded my own apartment so much that I could enter it fully and easily and move around inside. The more I expanded its dimensions, the more the main hole decreased. Exhaustion overcame me. Some time that night, I collapsed into a deep sleep.

I was awakened by the squawking of crows, the crunching sounds of them landing on top of the banana leaves strewn all around above. It was the daytime, sunny and clear of clouds or rain. I lay there in the dust, reluctant to rise. The sounds of birds, the sunlight; it was all more beautiful to me than it had ever appeared before, even as I lay separated from most of it by tons of earth. I savored the most pleasant rest that I could ever remember experiencing.

I thought about how wonderful my meal had been, the night before. Such pleasure and appreciation for God's undeserved gifts, arising from such misery! I may never in my life experience so pleasant a sleep as the one spent in that awful hole! It's a mystery that has convinced me that there is very little in life that we really consider. These moments of respite in a time of terror have given me a lasting appreciation for those small things.

I labored to my feet and stretched out my stiff limbs. It was time to continue working. Able to dig more efficiently in the sunlight, I set out to finish as much of the work as possible before dark.

By the time I could no longer read my watch, I had reduced the depth of the main hole to only three and a half meters. I was losing the ability to make out the form and outline of my cave; I dug faster, using up the last remaining light. My labors distracted me from Gaetan approaching; by the time I heard his footsteps on the banana leaves, I panicked and bolted into my newly-expanded cave, neglecting even to cover the entrance with its plastic curtain.

Gaetan's familiar voice floated down, whispering that he had brought Jeanne.

I had no time to climb to the surface and help her down. Gaetan was already beginning to lower her down into the pit by her arms. He let her down gradually, and I positioned myself as best I could to catch her. I heard an "oh!" from her as he released his grip and she fell. I bent my head down and attempted to cushion her fall, feeling a sharp blow to my back. We fell crumpled into a heap on the ground. I thought for a moment that I had broken my spine.

Though hurting, I could still move. I pulled myself to my feet and helped up Jeanne, who seemed to be alright as well. The utter darkness of the pit, combined with her fall, had thrown her into a state of shock.

"Where are we? Where are we? I can't breathe!" I whispered to her to calm her, and she called my name, as if to be sure that a familiar face was near.

"Are you hurt by the fall?" she asked.

"No. And you don't have anything broken?"

"I'm fine. How are we going to survive in here? We are burying ourselves alive...please; we have to get out of here..."

I thought that she might be amused by our "apartment". As she talked I slipped quietly into it. She groped for me in the darkness.

101

"Charles! Charles! What's going on? Where are you, am I going crazy?"

I reappeared, as if by magic. "No, you aren't crazy. I'm here."

"Where did you go?" she asked. "You frightened me! It's like some kind of witchcraft."

I smiled. "I went to make sure that my princess' rooms are ready. Now let's leave the living room and visit my private apartments."

"What apartments?"

I held her arm and led her into the crevice by the stairs that I had carefully made the whole afternoon, to make access to the room easier.

The new hole was spacious enough for me to sit inside, with my back against the farthest wall, and invite Jeanne to sit in front of me. I had spread the bag out on the ground there, so that we could lie down on it and not directly in the dirt. I showed her how we could lie down to sleep here, shifting our bodies so as to avoid aches and cramps. I helped her relax and breathe deeply to stay calm. My pride at being able to show off my work had overcome my exhaustion.

A critical problem was her allergies, aggravated by the cold wind and moisture. As the night grew chillier, she began to sneeze frequently. Neighbors would certainly be alerted to a suspicious presence inside this hole!

We were forced to squeeze her nose and face with her head-wrap every time she was about to sneeze. After a few such painful incidents, we despaired that it would be impossible to continue on this way. Her allergies were worse than usual, but we dared not let her be heard sneezing even once. She began to desperately will herself not to sneeze, fearing the unpleasant suppression technique.

We thanked God for another small victory when her sneezing subsided and stopped completely! It was not only the end of her sinusitis attacks that night, but permanently. She never suffered another one.

Chapter 5
Living Underground

"...the use of the term 'genocide' has a very precise legal meaning, although it's not strictly a legal determination. There are other factors in there as well."

-Christine Shelley, U.S. State Department Spokesperson, when asked whether the Rwandan situation was, in fact, genocide
April 28, 1994

We battled to stay busy and optimistic as the reality of our dreary new world sank in. We had no way of knowing how long we would be forced to wait here, or how our ordeal would end.

We gathered some soft clay from what had been piled down in the pit from my digging, and scattered it along the bottom of our private room, to create a soft layer for when we slept. I dug a little more along the top of the crevice to create more space.

Despite our best efforts, fear and the cold made sleep difficult. We didn't dare to speak to one another, never knowing who might be wandering nearby. Insects climbed over us and buzzed around our ears. From time to time I whispered an encouraging word to Jeanne, who suffered greatly. The fear and distress from the past several days were now combined with a maddening monotony. We were prisoners locked in a tiny cell, tormented by the meager rations of wind and sun that reached down to us. Cold racked us in the nighttime; heat in the day.

After the first evening and morning we were already consumed by hunger. Our flagging spirits were revived when Gaetan brought us food in a plastic pouch, lowered down on a rope. Two miserable nights later, he came again, whispering assurances that he didn't plan to abandon us. It seemed to me that he found it difficult to safely approach our hole, especially without the cover of the banana plantation.

Our lives became an exercise in spiritual survival; a struggle to cling to hope and sanity. We wrestled in equal measure with fear of capture, paranoia, boredom, isolation, and the maddening silence we were forced to keep. Our minds kept returning to Gaetan's next visit, anticipating fresh water, a meal, and perhaps a word of news about the war. No hostile person or curious passerby approached our hole for four days, though every noise froze us in fear.

We trusted Gaetan, and I assured myself that he would return to us again as soon as possible. Then two more days and nights passed, and he had not come. The only reminder that anyone was left in the world came from the distant sounds of mortars and rifles, telling us nothing but that the fighting over Kigali continued.

Our hunger, and especially our thirst, intensified when a third full day passed without eating or drinking. April rains occasionally showered us, but we had no container to collect the water, and were able to drink precious little. Still no visit from our benefactor. Competing thoughts warred within me. *Is it time yet to panic and try anything? Could Gaetan have fallen into trouble, perhaps on account of his brother Fidele? Could he be dead? How long could we remain here before beginning to die slowly of dehydration?* I considered myself a fighter– someone who was up to any challenge. But the past few days' events had humbled me; on several occasions, I had avoided death entirely by providence. I learned an important lesson on that third night without food– I prayed, and entrusted our future to God, rather than waiting until the moment of desperation.

I found it encouraging just reclaiming the name of God in my mind. Three days and nights had passed. Gaetan seemed to have vanished from the face of the earth. If we were going to try climbing out of this hole, we would have to do so while we still had the strength.

God, You've shown me that You are faithful in moments like these. I know that for some reason You have helped us. I don't know why. We are no better than those who have died. Please save us again before it's too late...

That evening we decided that in the middle of the night, we would brave the ascent from the pit and try to find food and water. We sat down to wait for the evening to grow still.

At about eight o'clock, we heard faint footsteps approaching. By this time we could recognize Gaetan only by the sound of his stealthy advance towards the hole. He was back! And with him, a new surge of hope!

I rejoiced inwardly and thanked God. What joy amid suffering! And to know that sustenance was coming right at the limits of what we could endure! As before, a plastic bag descended haltingly at the end of a rope, filled with beans, potatoes, and meat, mixed with a well-prepared chili sauce.

Our doubts and fears evaporated along with the heavenly steam that arose from that plastic bag! As always, not wanting to introduce our mud-covered hands into the bag, we carefully opened it wide and plunged our mouths in, eating like dogs. We devoured it with a great appetite, to the last crumb. The hunger of over three days dissipated; we felt strength and life return to us. We didn't dare to speak to Gaetan, nor he to us, but I started to wonder what had prevented him from coming sooner. Would it be another three days or more before we ate or drank again?

During the fifteen days and fifteen nights that we would live hidden deep underground, it was always in this bestial way, like dogs, that we fed. Every day we trembled, surrounded by the rumble of heavy weapons, rifles, machine guns, and grenades, fearful that the war might break out upon us. We could hear the Interahamwe shouting to one another, chasing down enemies. Sometimes we heard them singing, celebrating their victories over enemies massacred in homes, in the hills, or herded into churches and schools. It felt as if we were in a hallucination, or witnessing the end of the world.

All of our comings and goings consisted of sitting or lying curled up inside our tiny apartments, or moving into the main hole dug by Gaetan, sitting or standing, stretching and relaxing as best we could.

Our sweltering days and miserable nights blended into one another.

By the 26th of April, our discomfort had become unbearable. The sounds of war had ceased two days earlier, and we were haunted by the maddening silence as much as we had been by the noise. It had been another three days and nights since Gaetan's last visit, and our dizzying hunger had returned. Worse, heavy rains fell throughout the day, and the hole– and especially our tiny apartment– were flooded.

We had no choice but to stand upright in the pit, wading in mud. The water rose slowly and terribly, first to our knees, and then to our waists. When in answer to our prayers the downpour finally ended, we were forced to continue standing in filthy water, waiting in anguish to be able to kneel or sit once again, as it gradually seeped into the ground. We stood in anxious silence for hours before our secret hiding place became available once again, at about six o'clock in the evening. Until then, we were in constant fear, exposed to anyone who might pass by.

We could now kneel and rest our legs a bit, but the night had grown cold and our clothes were heavy with water and dirt. Both of us trembled from head to toe; I could not feel my legs or feet. Jeanne could stand it no longer, and suggested to me that I head to the surface and have a look around for a hiding place in the fresh air. I obstinately insisted that we wait longer before taking such a gamble, though I really didn't know what held me back. I longed to be in the dry grass as much as she did, even at the risk of my life, but secretly I held out hope that Gaetan would surprise us again, at the last possible minute.

He seemed to have completely disappeared. We had heard no voices or sounds from the direction of his house. One more night in this freezing wet prison would likely kill us. By eight o'clock, our minds were made up. I couldn't lose time counting on the arrival of Gaetan any longer. I would return to the surface, and find a way to bring Jeanne up too.

The walls of our pit had become slippery and unstable. My first few attempts to climb to the top ended in slides, and falls into the mud. The night was pitch-black; for the last two days we had not even seen the light of the moon or stars. I stretched myself and scrambled up the pit walls again, this time reaching the level where I suspected the surface was.

Instead of a welcome blast of fresh air and dry land, I slammed unexpectedly into a wooden ceiling. Large, heavy pieces of lumber, connected by barbed wire, blocked the exit!

It could only have been Gaetan who must have covered our hole while we slept. Had it been to protect us? Still bracing myself against the pit's walls, I used the last of my strength to try and move the wooden beams aside. Trunks from the banana trees were laid over them; they shook as I grunted and shoved, but the beams barely moved. I gave up and returned to my wife, exhausted. She had prepared herself to be hiding alone in the hole for some time, and was surprised by my sudden return.

"What happened? Why are you back?"

"There are big wood pieces blocking the exit and I can't lift them. They are very heavy for me."

I had begun to panic at the prospect of being caged underground, but now forced myself to make a show of confidence for Jeanne's sake, and for mine. We could not accept that we were completely trapped here. We would find a way to escape.

"Oh, you have to do something," she despaired, "If we are going to die, it cannot be here!" She was overcome and began to cry.

I felt my own nerves about to give way as well. Her cries compelled me to try to escape the hole once again. It would have to be done tonight, before the breaking of the fourth day. Though we still didn't know exactly what we would do once free, we were desperate, sickly and ravaged by hunger.

I carefully made the climb once more. I planted my feet along the pit walls, and felt the rough wood above me for the best grip. I braced myself and placed my arm from hand to elbow in the space between beams.

For a minute or two I pushed and heaved, surprised at how little the beams separated from one another. There was no point in continuing to try pushing. I thought instead that I could punch a space in between them and perhaps reach my arm through. I breathed deeply and prepared myself to give the most powerful blow with my elbow that I could.

I risked accompanying my strike by a sharp exhalation: the *tsuki*, accompanied by a cry, the *kiyai*. I struck in between two of the pieces of wood. The effect seemed beyond what my remaining strength could ever have yielded! I felt the beams give way to either side of my forearm. For a moment I rested and regained composure, then felt along the ceiling above me to see what damage I had done. I could reach my arm up into the narrow space I'd created, and feel my way to the top of the beams in the darkness, where I came to realize the reason why they had been so unmoving. They were connected by metal plates attached with nails.

Ah! This man has buried us alive, I thought. Why? I couldn't believe that he would do so in bad faith. I stabilized myself and made sure that I was supported. Extending my arm as far as possible up between the beams, I was able to reach one of the banana tree-trunks and shove it aside. It was a more difficult task to remove the wooden beams, twisting and pulling on the metal plates to detach them from one another.

With a lot of trouble, (and far more noise than I was comfortable with), I soon had removed enough wood to place my right shoulder, as well as my arm, through the gap. I awkwardly shifted and rotated my body, reaching as far across the wooden ceiling as possible to be able to continue my work. After disconnecting and pushing away the third beam, I could fit my entire torso out, dangerously pushing away with my feet from the walls of the pit and leaning all of my weight across the remaining beams. My thinness and the weight that I'd lost, at that moment, became an advantage that might have saved my life from a deadly fall!

Bent upon my elbows, I scrambled out of the hole. I was in the open air! It was incredible! A miracle! Just one hour earlier I had not been able to feel my hands and feet. I had just spent seventy hours with nothing to eat, and was dizzy with hunger. To have made it this far was beyond my capabilities.

So overjoyed was I to have reached the surface, I forgot for a moment to even fear capture. At the corner of Gaetan's house I spied a drum filled with rainwater, and satisfied myself for a full minute, collapsing on the lawn, my thirst quenched. For several minutes I lay across the wonderfully clean grass, exhausted. I nearly fell asleep before I remembered Jeanne, still faint and sickly below. *I cannot leave her there any longer. Either we get out together, or we die together...*
The thought of Jeanne wasting away from cold and hunger shocked me back into wakefulness. *Not the time to lie down and die! You have enough strength left to find a way to get Jeanne out, too! You're living because God wants you to be...so find the solution...*

I faced every direction; there was neither sight nor sound of anyone awake. I began to think about a way to lift Jeanne out of the hole. A rope...some kind of long cord...if I had such a thing I could wrap it around Jeanne, underneath her arms. I could tie the other end to my leg. She could follow the order of my footholds and ascend behind me. Once I reached the surface, I could use the rope to pull her the rest of the way out...
With this rough idea of an escape plan in my mind, I went to look for a rope. There was nothing in the banana plantation. I crept underneath the shadow of Gaetan's house, which was dark and still. I felt my way through the corners of the storehouse for a rope, but found nothing. I circled the house, searching in every place where I thought a rope might be kept. There was not even so much as a clothesline on the grounds. After several minutes of hunting, and exposing myself to discovery and danger, I retreated back into the darkest area behind the house, disappointed. What to do now?

A solution sprang to mind that, to me, seemed even more effective than a mere rope. Jeanne's Dutch wax loincloths!

I crept back to the hole, where she was anxiously waiting. "Where are your loincloths?" I whispered as softly as I could.

"What loincloths?"

At that moment, I saw no other thing in the world as valuable as these loincloths.

"The loincloths that you wore around you when you ran to Dr. Alphonse's house...when you were disguised as a servant?"

"Yes. I wear them on top of my jeans."

"Remove them and give them to me."

There were three pieces. Three strips of cloth that I now considered the most priceless treasure that God had ever given me. They were the sum of our life, and they were going to save Jeanne.

As Jeanne tossed me the three dirty rags, I unspooled them and firmly tied them end to end, making a cloth cord of five meters. I tightened the knots so that they could not be broken, then slid and tumbled down the hole to Jeanne.

She was slumped against the black soil of the side of the hole. I helped her to her feet.

"What are you going to do?" she asked.

"Lift your arms, no time to explain now. Don't be afraid."

She was nervous, but hopeful. I thought making the attempt quickly would be more effective than talking over our plans. I started carefully tying the loincloths rope around the level of her chest.

"Please, follow me exactly. Otherwise we will not succeed."

The way to climb back to the surface was to place the left and right feet in the small gaps dug into either side of the pit. One step at a time, we would rise. Jeanne was not able to reach both sides at once– she would at times be totally suspended in the air by the cloth rope. I would have to hold her up as best I could those times.

The rope was not long enough to reach all the way to the top of the pit; I couldn't climb first and then assist Jeanne up. Instead I tied the cloth tightly above my right foot, and climbed once again. Taking a quick look around to make sure the area was clear, I sat down at the edge of the hole, my foot still hanging down. The fabric had tightened. I lodged my left foot firmly into one of the support holes embedded in the wall of the hole, said a brief, silent prayer for safety, and pulled, assisting Jeanne as she climbed.

The cloth stretched and tightened, but didn't tear. She left the ground, clinging to the supports as I loudly whispered instructions. A single slip of her feet, or of mine, could pull us both down forcefully to the ground. I strained back and upwards with all of my might, drawing some of the cloth in, hand over hand, each time Jeanne found a foothold. All the while I was giving orders as in a military operation:

"Now...this way...hang on there for a minute...okay, climb...you've got it..."

"Oh, it's harming me very badly, I can't breathe."

"Just a few more meters and you'll be out. There's a foothold. Stop there and rest for a second..."

By this time I was very nearly shouting. If we failed, there would likely not be another chance for Jeanne to escape. I had forgotten the danger that I was putting us both in by raising my voice.

Soon I could hear Jeanne writhing near the surface, clawing towards the light with all of her remaining strength. I grunted in pain as I reached down towards my right ankle, where my lower leg was pinned down to the ground by the tightly-wrapped cloth. I grasped it beneath my foot, where just underneath, Jeanne was struggling to breathe. I could not relieve her– only pull her to the surface to end her ordeal as quickly as possible. I strained until her silhouette emerged from the abyss. As soon as I could grasp her hand, I lunged backwards in the dark. We collapsed onto the grass together, Jeanne in tears.

Together in the open air! The joy and relief of that moment was enough to make us forget that we would forfeit our lives if a single person saw us gasping there on the ground. We were rescued from the suffocating chasm that had, until then, been our salvation.

I rubbed the face of my watch on the grass where I lay, clearing away the caked mud until I could make out the time in the dim light of the moon. It was four o'clock in the morning! Our struggle to return to the surface had taken several hours altogether. I don't know how we did it. Time and time again, I had seen the claws of the devil, but also the unfailing hand of God. By now I was even beginning to trust and expect it. Still sprawled, exhausted, next to that hole, I was filled with gratitude.

We must thank you once again. It's not by our strength, but by Your love and help. Thank you...thank you...

Somewhere, a rooster crowed. A new sunrise was coming. Now we had to find shelter, food, and water– but we had no idea where to go, and precious little time.

Gaetan had not been seen for four days. During that time our hole had mysteriously been covered and sealed– but it couldn't have been because he wanted us dead. If he intended to get rid of us, there had already been better chances to do so before now. I was convinced that he'd met with some difficulty. It was possible that he and his family had been killed, or were forced to flee for their lives. The thought was too horrible to entertain. In any event, we would approach his house and try to learn what we could.

Keeping to the shadows, we crept towards the front of the house. I quietly tested the door and found it locked. I leaned my ear against the door and listened. No sound. We did the same at the windows, but heard no snores, no signs of life. Could they be so deeply asleep?

There was nowhere else to go, and nothing remained but death back inside the pit from which we had come. Day was approaching. Increasingly desperate, we found the window of Gaetan's bedroom. I knocked on it cautiously. Taking an even greater risk, I knocked harder and even called out. There was no sound from within, and nothing was visible but utter darkness. It seemed as if no soul was inside.

Connected to the house was the annex that served as an apartment housing Gaetan's nephew, Modesto. The door there was made of a thinner, more fragile wood. If it were also unoccupied, I could force my way inside. Even if Gaetan and his family were truly gone, we might at least find a hiding place in the annex. With only minutes until sunrise, it was our last resort.

I looked over the locked door. It was padlocked on the outside– further proof that the place was abandoned. The lock was small and attached to a thin hinge on the door. After nervously checking in every direction to be sure we were still unwatched, I struck the door twice as hard as I could, surveying the area again after it gave way, for fear that the sound might have awakened someone. The night was unusually devoid of the usual distant war-sounds, making my noise all the more cringe-inducing.

For one horrified moment, I scanned the rooms inside fearing the worst– that the annex was still occupied by Gaetan's dangerous nephew. My eyes were already well-adjusted to the darkness. Modesto's wing of the house seemed to have been abandoned in a hurry– it had been left in an unkempt state; clothes strewn about, the bed unmade. I made a quick but thorough search before returning outside to Jeanne to assure her that the place was empty. We hurried inside, groping our way through the living room and into the tiny bedroom. From the open window there, the remains of the banana plantation were visible, and the entrance to our underground hiding place. I said a last farewell to it...our home of three horrible weeks.

114

Jeanne robbed me of my musings when she shouted that something had passed over her foot. It was a rat, tunneling through the piles of clothes and refuse on the floor. Her yell of surprise filled us both with fear once again, and we stood motionless for a full minute, listening for a sign that someone had heard us.

Silence all around. It really seemed as if we were now the only souls still living in the whole district of Remera. That would certainly explain why we hadn't been captured, in spite of all of the commotion we'd made getting ourselves here. How could we learn what had actually happened in the last four days? Cornered with my thoughts, I began to wonder if we had made the right decisions that night. The darkness outside was retreating already, and we still had nothing to eat. We would have to suffer for another twelve hours at least before venturing outside to scavenge for food, and that was assuming that we were not intruded upon by then. We weren't even in the relative safety of Gaetan's own rooms anymore— we had instead trapped ourselves in the apartment of a man who wanted us dead.

Our one comfort, and not a small one, was the double bed in that room, with its wonderful foam mattress and multicolored sheets. We peeled off our dirt-covered clothes and shook them off as best we could, then resigned ourselves to whatever fate would be ours. If we were going to die today, we would enjoy a luxurious sleep first.

Since that first awful morning on April 7, we had been driven to exhaustion physically, spiritually, and emotionally, with little to no respite. There was a foolish joy in our decision to collapse in sleep, having done what little we could to prolong our lives. We had become aware of God's constant presence with us, and were at peace. My sleep was instant, and dreamless.

Weeks of forced alertness had trained me to start nervously at the slightest sound, and so I was awakened, after the better part of twelve hours spent unconscious, by the most dreaded noise: that of someone stomping around the grounds. Footsteps on the banana plantation, rummaging around the pieces of wood and tree-trunks blocking the entrance to the hole.

I bolted upright in the bed; it was now the afternoon. My movement awakened Jeanne, who joined me in fearful paralysis there. The footsteps were of someone searching the yard.

I had sloppily replaced the beams and other debris around the hole, but it would be clear to anyone searching there that it had been used as a hiding place, and that its occupants had fled. The footsteps came towards the house, and paused at the door, perhaps noticing the damage that I had done to the lock. It was Modesto himself; or perhaps a member of the Interahamwe paramilitary, claiming the place as his own.

After a few moments of silence, suddenly a loud *bang!* And then another, as our hearts leapt from our chests. He was breaking in, just as I had done myself, the night before. I had returned the hinge and lock to their previous state as best I could before collapsing onto the bed, but the once-broken hinge gave way easily. There was a loud crash, and we were no longer alone in the house.

I stole over to the bedroom door, as Jeanne slipped into hiding behind the bed. I was cornered and desperate, and now ready to defend our lives by force. I might, at least, have the element of surprise. I could attack quickly and hope to incapacitate the intruder before any help could come to him. I coiled myself in the shadows at the side of the door, ready to strike.

The door swung open, revealing a figure in a long, black coat. He stepped forwards, passing me, and allowing me to gain a stranglehold on him from directly behind. I was surprised by the strength that the will to live had granted my emaciated body as I tightened my fingers on his throat, trying to muffle his cries with my other arm. I was no soldier, and felt a split-second's hesitation as I feared that I might be about to take a life for the first time.

In that moment, the muffled cry of my victim struck me as familiar. I realized that he was none other than our benefactor, Gaetan. I released him, baffled, and let loose a barrage of apologies and excuses as he staggered backwards.

"Gaetan, I am really sorry…I thought it was an attack by someone. Are you alright? Forgive me, I am so sorry..."

He was confused and sputtering, rubbing the place on his neck where I had sunk my fingers. I stood and watched him awkwardly, quite ashamed of myself. Jeanne emerged from behind the bed, a blanket wrapped over her shoulders. She joined me in making amends as Gaetan haltingly regained his voice.

"Aaggh...your husband...strangled me...was about to break my throat...I can still barely breathe."

"Charles? How could he dare to do this to you?" Jeanne offered her apologies for me. My discomfort increased.

"Gaetan, I really regret stran... doing that. I implore your forgiveness."

"Never mind it." Gaetan regained most of his composure. "You didn't do it on purpose. What I really cannot believe...is that you were foolish enough to hide in Modesto's house! Do you not realize that you could kill us all? Lucky for you, I've preceded him here. If he'd arrived before me, he would no doubt enjoy being the one to catch the elusive Charles Mwumvaneza. And we'd all be dead..." The look of panic in his eyes was one that I had learned well– it was the look of a man who could soon lose all that he loved.

As he finished speaking he drew from his cloak a large plastic bag. It was a generous portion of rice and meat. I was unable to hold back my tears, affected as I was by the compassion of this man towards us.

For the next several minutes we worked together to return Modesto's apartment to its exact former state. Gaetan then hurried us into his own house, where we learned the risks that he'd endured, traveling several kilometers just to bring us food. The sealing of our hole with wood had been to cover it, hiding it from any spy who might have come by during his absence.

"Charles," he said, "forgive me for not notifying you. The FPR and the Rwandan Armed Forces are warring over Kigali. The FPR nearly took Kimironko, and the FAR were beginning to retreat. We had to close up our shop and flee to Nyandugungu; the rebel fire was beginning to reach here. If they were to take this area, my family and I would be finished."

I cursed my own skepticism and the doubts that I had thought towards him, taken once again by his bravery.

"The government regained their position," he went on, "and I took the opportunity to bring food back and check on you. I know how much you have suffered these last few days, but understand that the situation was impossible. Everyone in Kigali is on edge now. It seems that whatever happens here, one of us is going to end up dead. Perhaps both of us."

Living in a war zone with no malice towards anyone, then, Gaetan– a Hutu– had risked a thousand dangers to keep us fed and safe. I had little to say in response.

"Many thanks, brother. If God so wills that we remain alive, I will never forget all you did for us."

"If you want to do me a favor, then," he replied, "you must tell me who drew you out from that hole. Modesto my nephew is beginning to suspect that we are hiding someone. You are rather high on the Interahamwe's list; they really want to kill you. Anyone who knows that you are here holds our lives in their hands. Who is it? Who else is helping you? You really must tell us."

"No need to worry. Nobody helped us out. We did it ourselves."

"This is not the time for jokes, Charles. The more time that passes, the greater the danger. The names, please."

I had to recount in detail the method by which we climbed out of the pit ourselves. Gaetan was left once more shaking his head in disbelief, but he was satisfied.

"Such impossible tenacity...well, now you must rest here for a minute. We have to think of a solution to this problem..." I wondered exactly what he meant.

As we savored every bite of the wonderful, life-saving meal that Gaetan had so boldly won for us, he brought a single mattress and set in in the corner of the living room. A pile of blankets was brought for Jeanne, and for three more hours we slept, grateful and contented.

I awoke to see Jeanne already awake, sitting upright and well-rested, in a circle with Gaetan's wife and children. Gaetan himself was pacing back and forth around the house, sometimes stopping to hold a secret council with Dianne. His regular peaceful demeanor had given way to distress and agitation. I smiled towards Jeanne as we relished the comfort of our surroundings, kept warm by the *imbaba*– the cooking pot, in the center of the room. I could not tell what exactly our hosts were discussing, either from their words or from their body language, except that it was nothing pleasant.

At about 9:45 that evening, we were invited to come to the dining table. On one side was served a mixture of potatoes, beans, and a batter made from cassavas. On the other side, a tureen filled with meat spiced with tomato, green pepper and chili sauce. What joy, shame, pleasure, fear, love, and worry all came with that delicious meal, shared with friends and surrounded by enemies! After the better part of a month, it was still disquieting to think that we were fugitives in our own neighborhood, and that our host couple and their children could die for sharing a dinner with us that we might have enjoyed noisily, and in public, only weeks ago.

I meekly inquired about the fate of Gaetan's brother, Fidele. Gaetan seemed unwilling to discuss the subject; he only remarked that Fidele had found another hiding place. Our two rescuers then excused themselves for a moment. After a few minutes during which we feasted in silence, Gaetan returned, and asked me how my health was holding up. How did I feel?

It was the usual Rwandan way of approaching a delicate subject by coming around to it gradually, after a great deal of small talk. I was soon to find out what sort of future was in store for us.

"I think I feel quite better now, and thank you so much for the kindness of this afternoon. We're both so grateful that you came to bring us food. Without you, we would certainly have died."

"Well, Charles, the problem now is that they are looking for you everywhere. I don't know what role you must have played in the FPR to cause them to be so relentless about finding you, but they aren't giving up. Everywhere they're talking about how they must kill you at any cost! There is no doubt that if they find out we hid you, my family and I will all die.

"My nephew is even starting to suspect us. It is no longer possible for you to stay here– not even in the hole outside. This is not a safe place for you anymore. You must find another place to hide."

Another place to hide! It was the same as a death sentence from a judge. What other place was there?

"Gaetan, please, if you will, do everything possible to think of another safe hiding place for us. We don't wish to endanger you for another day, but to wander away would be the same as surrendering to these killers. Without your help we won't last long."

"My dear friend, I did everything in my power, but now I can do nothing. More than twenty families we know, by my count, have lost their lives already for being suspected Tutsi sympathizers. That's in our neighborhood alone."

He leaned forward, and his voice became softer still. "We have two friends– Gatete and Papa Fils– whom we have taken into our confidence. They cannot shelter you in their homes; they are being closely monitored by their neighbors. But if you need anything else, they might help in some way. That is the most we can do."

I seized upon one last hope. "My family is in Kabeza. I have two brothers there, Benoit and Guillaume. And cousins. I know that it's quite far, but if you can just think of a way to take me there..."

Gaetan's face revealed everything to me before he could speak the dreadful words.

"I am sorry, Charles. They are all dead."

It is a terrible enough thing to hear of the murder of loved ones; worse still to be denied a chance to properly mourn them. Gaetan seemed to understand this; he placed his hand upon my shoulder comfortingly, but firmly, as if to remind me that there was no time to yield to emotions. He quickly brought the exchange back to the matter at hand.

"Why don't you ask your friend Pastor Franco to hide you?"

"He is still in Kigali?"

"Oh yes, he has a large fenced house. He is a family friend of yours, yes?"

"Of course, we were always very close to him. His wife is like a sister to me; we knew each other since childhood. We looked after his children when he traveled abroad."

"Yes, I heard that you were the one to receive him at the airport. You should try to send a message to him. He is a minister, and I think he would take the risk of hiding you."

Good news at last! I latched onto the new hope of finding safety at Pastor Franco's house. While most ministers were accused of sympathizing with Tutsis and had fled or been killed, Pastor Franco, our friend, was still in Kigali!

Better still, Gaetan explained to me that Franco's house and family were under protection. If we could only get inside unnoticed, we could hide in safety from anyone hunting us.

Gaetan agreed that before seeing us away, we would make an attempt to contact Pastor Franco, in a way that would not point back to Gaetan's own family. I asked a sheet of paper and a pen and I wrote a quick note addressed to Franco:

Dear brother Franco and family,

By his goodness and mercy, God has kept us alive. My wife and I have been in hiding, but our conditions have been unbearable. Everyone is hunting us for no reason. Still, day after day we are experiencing the grace of our God, and we believe He will deliver us.

Jeanne and I hope this message will reach your hands. We no longer have any place to go. Please, if you can, be so generous as to give us a hiding place on your property until peace is restored– even if it is something as small as a storehouse or cellar. No doubt you don't need us to tell you how we believe God will bless you for such noble kindness, and we will be indebted to you with our lives.

Please respond soon,

Charles and Jeanne Mwumvaneza

P.S. My wife is in a pitiful hygienic state, as we have been hiding in the ground for weeks. She would be most grateful if you could provide her with the items described below. You could send them through the carrier of this note.

I listed the hygienic items desperately needed by Jeanne, and handed the letter over to Gaetan. We thought that if Franco were to give us the items requested, it would be a good sign that he was able and willing to help us.

Their daring plan was as follows: Gaetan and his two kindly friends, Papa Fils and Gatete, would pay the pastor a visit and attempt to speak with him alone, away from any officials who might be around the house. They would then slip him the letter, sealed and with Franco's name on the envelope, claiming to merely have found it. If the letter were somehow discovered by the Interahamwe, Gaetan and company might still be able to deny having me in their protection, though the danger was great.

It was already very late in the evening, and Gaetan wasted no time slipping out the door and into the night, where Gatate and Papa Fils waited for him, ready to begin the short but treacherous journey to see the minister, and leaving us alone with only our prayers.

We sat and listened for their return. Our hope was that their absence would be a long one, signifying that the pastor was gathering the items we needed, or perhaps making arrangements with our friends for our safe passage into his home. I tried not to dare to imagine the two of us curling up in a new, secure hiding place with the Pastor, enjoying a full night's sleep at last.

When the threesome returned relatively soon, our hopes faded, and then vanished completely once we could read the discouragement upon their faces.

Papa Fils broke the silence. "That man," he paused, quite angry, "is no pastor. He does not have the heart of a human being."

"No, he is a true monster instead," added Gatete.

"What did he say?" I was crushed.

"He told us that he has no friendship with *inyenzi* traitors of your kind, and that you would have to die and pay the price for your crimes."

"He even had the nerve to ask where you were, intending to hand you over to his military friends," added Gaetan. "I very quickly guessed his intentions and was careful not to reveal anything. We told him that we didn't know where you were; only that we got the letter from a young boy who asked us for your address, saying it was for you. We didn't know the boy, we said, or the meaning of the letter."

"Franco seems to have turned in many an unfortunate Tutsi to the FAR," Gatete added. "I saw that we were about to be in a lot of trouble; he was getting very suspicious. So I told him, 'I have seen this boy playing with your children at home. I think he is a classmate of theirs.' Then he settled down! He didn't want to be found to have any connection with a Tutsi in hiding."

There was a moment of discomforting silence. Papa Fils hung his head sorrowfully. "We have done all we can, I am afraid. Go with God; we'll pray that He continues to keep you safe."

There was nothing left to say or do, except watch Gatete and Papa Fils vanish away into the darkness outside. We would probably never see them again.

Many times since that awful night, Jeanne and I had second-guessed whether it was possible that the Reverend Franco, our friend, could really have been capable of being ensnared in such hatred. It was easier to be in denial about such things. We wondered whether events had truly transpired at Franco's house the way we'd been told.

Long, long afterwards, I would meet a witness to that meeting at Franco's– a man who had been hiding nearby, overhearing the conversation between Gatete, Papa Fils, Gaetan, and Franco on the minister's front lawn. It was none other than Protogène– our friend who'd been visiting my house when the militia first attacked, destroyed and looted it. He, also, had narrowly survived the genocide of 1994, and told me the tale of his escape.

Having helped to build our house, he knew every inch of it. As the Interahamwe stormed their way inside, he managed to climb up into a concrete deck above our bedroom closet. As he explained it to me, he knew that this hiding place was safe, even if fired on through the ceiling.

124

Proto worked in construction; late that night, he had left his hiding place in the roof and fled towards an unfinished house he was working on– a house right across from the home of Franco. While in hiding there, he had seen our three neighbors approach and talk with Franco, privately rejoicing to learn that I had also managed to cheat death. The meeting between Franco and our three friends, unfortunately, happened just the way that they had described it to me. Protogène confirmed this. Franco's treatment of us was only one of many betrayals that I was to endure from my own Rwandan countrymen.

The pain of Franco's rejection of us must have registered on our faces. Gaetan meekly offered a suggestion of how we might begin our journey.

"There are a couple of abandoned houses nearby– Hutu houses, houses that have not been demolished. You might escape notice hiding near one of them."

"Whose houses?" I thought that if we were captured on an abandoned property, at least no one would die on our account.

"Ramiyaka, the truck driver, for one. He was away in Kenya, taking a delivery to Mombasa, when the killing started. He is Hutu, but I think that he'll stay away from Kigali until the fighting is over. Also, Nabara. You know him, I think. As soon as the president died, he went to the Kanombe military camp. Some of the soldiers there are his friends. He has not returned."

The idea of trying to hide at one of these two houses was an unpleasant one. We'd be surrounded by the cottages of northern-Rwandan refugees, men who had lost their homes, livelihoods and loved ones to Tutsi soldiers. They were now exacting revenge against any innocent Tutsi they could find: men, women, and children. Hiding in the midst of them would put us in constant danger. Even an abandoned house was no place to hide; the owners might return, or opportunistic neighbors could come looking for something to steal. The FAR and the militia men could occupy any home as they pleased.

But we were abusing the generosity of Gaetan with every passing moment. I told him that my wife and I were ready to depart. We prayed together, asking for God's blessing over the family that had so willingly obeyed God's command to love their neighbors, even at the cost of sheltering the so-called enemy. We committed ourselves into God's hands once again.

Gaetan kept watch over the area as we headed out directly towards the fences and gardens of those who hunted us by day. From henceforth there was no more place of refuge; no hole in which to hide. Only our pain and our faith.

Nabara's house was nearest to us. He had been a friendly neighbor of ours; our properties were close enough together that we had sometimes seen each other from our respective plots, and met to have a chat. Feeling as if eyes were watching us from every direction, we reached the stone wall and fence surrounding Nabara's place and crouched down in its shadow. We could look back and see Gaetan's front door; he had disappeared inside.

We huddled there beneath the wall for about an hour, listening and peering through the locked gate for any signs of life inside. If we stayed there, prostrate along the ground, we'd likely be seen by a night patrol, or by Interahamwe returning home from an evening spent carousing. We would have to take a chance and climb the fence, trusting that the house was truly unoccupied.

The difficulty would be getting Jeanne over the wall. Along the top of it was laid glass and other sharp debris. We whispered our counsels to each other, and I boosted her up to the top of the fence. As she slid up and over, I had no choice but to release her and wince at the noise as she dropped down onto the concrete inside.

She landed on her feet, and I quickly followed. Once again we huddled in the darkness, still as stones, making sure that our noise hadn't disturbed anybody. While we waited I observed that her hands and arms had several small cuts and scrapes from the broken glass.

The house and grounds seemed truly deserted. There were two sheds in the backyard along with the main house; all of them were locked. I went to every door and window, listening, as I had at Gaetan's, for the presence of any living soul. It was black and silent inside.

Drops of rain began to fall. It was about four or four-thirty in the morning. We'd have to make a decision before daybreak; whether to force our way in to one of the sheds, or perhaps try the main house. There was also an outdoor toilet in the backyard, though it offered little in the way of a hiding place. Whatever shelter we could find within the next hour, it would have to protect us all throughout the coming day. It was a deadly game of hide-and-seek we played there among the very dwelling-places of the Interahamwe.

I consulted with Jeanne. "Either we force this door and we enter, or we go to look over Ramiyaka's house instead."

"We should go there. Nabara never really inspired in me much confidence. If he or any of his relations come to this house, I don't think we would be spared. I would trust Ramiyaka before Nabara."

"But Ramiyaka is not there. He is on a trip to Mombasa. And if Claver, the housekeeper, is still there, I don't know if he would be willing to help us."

"I don't think Claver would do any harm to us. He is a gentle boy."

The idea of spying out Ramiyaka's house prevailed. His home was adjacent to Nabara's, separated only by barrier of eucalyptus trees surrounded by flowers. We reached the house with little difficulty. Rain was falling freely now, masking the sound of our footsteps, soaking our dirty clothes.

I looked over the black outline of this second house, as I had Nabara's. It seemed equally deserted. But my survey was interrupted by the sight of a man in a raincoat walking towards us along the street, and the sounds of snatches of singing.

We backed ourselves into the darkness along the stone wall and kept our eyes towards this new visitor. To our horror, he opened the mail gate in front of Ramiyaka's house, cheerfully singing and staggering with drink, holding gleaming objects in both hands. He walked directly past the front door and towards the annexes, in our direction. It was young Claver, the household servant of Ramiyaka, with two half-empty bottles in one hand and his weapon, a machete, in the other.

I decided that I would accost him before he came any nearer. If he had surrendered to hatred and become one of the Interahamwe himself, then at least I could face him without revealing Jeanne's presence. As reckless as it seemed, risking exposure for a chance at a secure hiding place was worth the danger.

I leaped out of my hiding place, gently calling him by name.

"Claver. Claver, it's me, Charles." He dropped the two bottles in surprise.

"Don't be afraid," I entreated him as he tightened his grip on the machete and faced me. "It's Charles. I have been in hiding. You know that we were always good friends with your boss. We are desperate, hoping that we could have a place to hide at your house." His expression did not change. I stepped closer.

"You know that we are not the enemy. I am Charles, Yves's father. We are Ramiyaka's friends. We've never done you any wrong. We're in great danger. Please, can you find a place to hide us in your house?"

He remained in a fighting stance in the pouring rain, weapon pointed towards me, saying nothing.

"Claver, don't do that to me. Please understand that I come peacefully, begging for your help."

I carefully stepped closer. He seemed to be peering into the darkness to better identify me.

"Who are you?"

"As I said, I am Charles; my wife is Jeanne. We have been running for our lives for weeks now. People are trying to kill us because they think that I am Tutsi. We thought that if we came here, perhaps our friend would be willing to help us. I know that you don't know us as well as Ramiyaka, but we are your friends. If you can save us from the killers, perhaps one day we will be able to show our gratitude to you."

He lowered his weapon, seeming to recognize me. But what hope I had was quickly replaced by fear.

"I don't care who you are, or whether you live or die. Doesn't mean anything to me. You'd better leave now, or it'll be the worse for you."

With this dismissive, he staggered back towards the door of the house, leaving me trembling and unsure. Would he report us? He wasn't hurrying to raise the alarm. Did it mean that he cared for our lives? Why, then, would he threaten and speak to me as he did? Was it because he was drunk? I decided I had to be sure he would not betray us. I walked after him through the rain, meeting him at the door as he fumbled with the keys.

"Claver," I begged, "I am sorry to bother you. Jeanne is with me. All this time we have been outside and in the rain. Our clothes are ruined and we have been dreadfully cold. As you can see, now we are soaked again. We will appreciate your generosity if you could only find us something to keep us warm."

Considering that we were dancing with death, the cold and rain hardly bothered me at the moment. But I thought that if Claver was willing to help us in even such a small matter, we could be sure that he wouldn't hand us over to the militia.

He looked me over. "If that's all you want, it won't be a problem, as long as you leave this place. Just wait a bit until I find my key."

Jeanne had boldly emerged from her hiding place and joined my side. As the inebriated Claver struggled to fit the correct key into the lock, she offered to help. He accepted, and she seized the moment to thank him a thousand fold for his kindness towards us. As the door at last opened and Claver stumbled inside, I marveled at the change in my wife, remembering how she had preferred to wait for death rather than venture out from Dr. Alphonse's home. How she had adapted to our horrible situation since then– and how admirably risen to the occasion!

We instinctively started to follow Claver into the shelter and safety of the empty house, but he wheeled around and refused to let us past the threshold.

"You cannot enter here. They could come at any time, day or night, without warning. You don't need me to tell you what would happen to me if they found you here."

I thought that Claver was softening towards us. Perhaps the liquor was wearing off. "True," I bargained, "but we're willing to hide anywhere. Couldn't you lock us in a room or closet, and make sure no one goes in?"

"Forget it," his tone made me feel as though we were testing his patience. "These thugs might have just been workmen or beggars before, but now they are the law. They've killed thousands of people. Rwanda is theirs. They have the right to search any house and do as they please to whomever they find. I'm telling you, these people are crazy. Forget about hiding here, I won't allow it."

We waited instead in the rain, until Claver returned and handed each of us a large, luxurious bath towel, newly laundered. I felt unworthy to sully such a splendid towel, as dirty as I was.

"Oh, we only needed something to shelter us from the cold. You don't have to waste towels of such high quality."

He chuckled. "We have no lack of towels or any other fine things at the moment. For all I know, they could be yours. Don't worry about me."

Then Claver had been participating in the looting of Tutsi homes. His voice became stern.

"Now then, leave at once. Don't come back." He gestured toward the way from which we had come. "The outhouse in Nabara's backyard is open. You can hide in there; maybe nobody finds you."

I grasped at one final way to gauge his faithfulness.

"Alright, we do not want to trouble you. But Claver, we have no way of getting any food. Would you be able to bring us something?"

"I don't have any food here. I've been eating at the restaurants. How would I get food for you?"

"I don't know, but we would be forever grateful if you could. It's alright though; we don't want to bother you."

He was silent for a moment. Then he lowered his voice.

"Fine. Be waiting for me in the toilet at Nabara's, and I'll see if I can find you something. Now go, quick, before someone sees you here."

He followed us with his eyes as we retreated, watching until we were beyond his property and no longer his problem.

The outdoor toilet was a tiny wooden structure, with a cold concrete slab for a floor, the toilet hole in its center. It was used mainly when there was a water shortage, and indoor bathrooms were off-limits. The smell of ammonia from the hole filled the place. We sat in the corner there, closest to the door and to fresh air. The rain outside had become a raging storm.

An hour passed, then two. It was only the storm clouds kept us in total darkness. Claver did not come, and we grew regretful that we'd revealed ourselves to him. He had provided us with the towels draped over our backs, relieving us from the cold; and yet he'd seemed so eager to be rid of us! No doubt he feared the Interahamwe more than God. He might choose to betray us. Worse still, he knew our exact location…

Storm or no storm, we would soon lose the benefit of dark skies. I was still pondering whether to run to a new hiding place, when Claver appeared at the outhouse door. He was covered from head to foot by a long raincoat, and said nothing. The wind, rain and thunder made all communication apart from shouting impossible anyway.

From his inside coat-pocket he drew two sardine cans and a pocketknife, which he used to awkwardly pry the cans open. Handing them to me, he wordlessly disappeared back into the storm, never to be seen again, like a providential angel.

Jeanne and I smiled at one another, rejoicing.

"Very mysterious boy," she whispered into my ear. Even inside the outhouse, the storm made her nearly inaudible.

Watching the sheets of rain fall outside, I thanked God again for our good fortune. As long as it rained, there would be no one out hunting for us. And we were relatively safe from watching eyes, behind Nabara's trees and walls.

I ventured out the flimsy door into the rain, removed my filthy clothes, and helped myself to a thorough shower provided by the heavens. It was a delightful gift, as the mud that had accumulated and dried on my skin and hair at last melted away, and I enjoyed it so completely that I did not notice at first that I had been joined by another. Jeanne was beside me.

"Better to catch pneumonia than to go another day with this filth of three weeks on me," she smiled.

The rain washed our stiff, muddy clothes as well. As we savored our cleansing shower, we forgot– for only a moment– that our lives were in terrible danger. Caution prevailed as soon as we could make out one another's features in the dim first light of morning.

We put on our wet clothes and slipped back into the outhouse with its suffocating ammonia smell, our spirits now revived. We sat down in opposing corners, covered ourselves with our gigantic new towels, and settled in to await our fates.

I was alone with my thoughts now– for the first time since Gaetan had told me that my brothers and cousins were dead. There was no escaping the sad and beautiful memories of them; the hours wrestling with rage, agony, love, and unrelenting tears. I was careful not to disturb Jeanne with my grief, and mourned silently, sobbing noiselessly. The bath towel provided by Claver became my sanctuary, and in it I memorialized the dearly departed Benoit and Dr. Guillaume, my brothers, commending their souls to the Father from inside that tiny chapel. It was the only wake that the injustice of the times would allow them.

I don't know for how many hours I wept and ached there, or at what hour I at last sighed into a miserable sleep. Jeanne woke me. It was now fully morning. Had she been able to find a bit of sleep too? I do not know, and I didn't ask.

This day was sure to be a difficult one. At best, we would suffer in nervous silence for sixteen hours, stuffed inside this foul-smelling shed, until late in the evening, when we could scavenge for food and decide whether to risk hunting for a better hiding place. At worst, someone would come snooping around Nabara's property, perhaps even to use the restroom.

Jeanne had slid over next to me. "Do you think that that boy will really not talk?" I whispered to her.

"No, I don't think he is capable of such a thing. I am more afraid of someone coming to use this outhouse."

"I agree with you. Claver would not have given us two fine towels and some food if he intended to get us killed. But it's frightening that he and so many others know that we are hiding around here..."

All day long, through the narrow slit of the open outhouse door, we continued to watch intently, expecting to see someone come through the main gate. Our greatest fear was that Nabara himself would return, and take up residence in his own house again.

The first day ended without incident. We decided to stay where we were that night, surviving off of the cans of sardines brought by Claver. After sunset, we whispered a prayer of thanksgiving together and slept peacefully.

By the second morning, the sun was shining brightly and the land had mostly dried. We sat listlessly in cramped silence as before.

Early in the afternoon the gate opened.

A woman unlocked the gate and headed straight into the backyard. I didn't know her name, but I recognized her as the wife of Claude, the Interahamwe neighbor who'd shined a flashlight into my hole in the banana plantation. She stopped at what must have been a small garden near our hiding place and knelt down to harvest vegetables.

We might have been delighted to learn that there was a food source within reach, if only we weren't in the company of a woman whose husband was desperate to kill us. We scarcely breathed, knowing that at any moment she might enter the restroom. Minutes later, a male voice was heard humming to himself at the gate. This new visitor opened it, and his footsteps approached us. We panicked inwardly, fearing that he had come to use the restroom, but instead he went to the vegetable garden, to talk to the woman as she worked. I thought that he might be Claude himself, until the woman's voice greeted him.

"Hello Mapida. You look very tired. It's because you are working so hard these days, isn't it?"

Mapida's name was one that I knew well. He was a friend and coworker of Nabara. Had he been alone, I might have called out to him for help, as I had done weeks ago with Gaetan. I had always known Mapida to be a kind and gentle neighbor, not the sort to get himself caught up in the sadism and avarice that had swept away Rwanda. He and Nabara were both from my hometown of Buganza, a place known for intermarriage and tolerance between Hutu and Tutsi.

I carefully crept up beside the tiny window of the outhouse, to spy on their conversation. I was hoping to collect some useful information, perhaps some news about the war. What I did hear, I certainly hadn't expected.

Mapida shared his experiences helping to hunt and kill *inyenzi* throughout the region of Remera, Kibagabaga and Kabeza. At times he described, with pleasure, the ignominious manner in which they had been slaughtered. This man was a distinguished killer among the Interahamwe.

Among the victims he named many of our dear friends. My cousin, Viviane, and her three children. Children thrown into a hole alive, to die slowly of heat and thirst. At last he shared with Claude's wife the fate of my childhood friend, David Twahirwa.

"That man gave us such a hard time," he spat. "We chased him out of his house and he ran like the wind. We were all out of breath. Might have gotten away, too, if he hadn't tried to take shelter at Major Kanika's house. The Major chased him– brave as can be– and caught him in the fields. He'll never run again now."

"It's a pity," said the woman, "he was always a very kind and sociable neighbor."

"Think before you speak! You're going to get yourself killed talking stupidity like that. There is no good Tutsi. They're hateful, greedy bigots, and if they had a chance they'd show no mercy to you. Remember that."

"And his wife and the children?"

"What do you think? We have to get rid of *all* of the Tutsi, for good this time. After we caught him we brought them all together, and threw them alive into the pit behind their house, tied up. We'd have been kinder and done it the usual way, but this man gave us a lot of trouble."

I felt tears streaming down my cheeks. Was it possible for a good man to do such things, and feel no compassion? And if Mapida could become such a savage, was anyone really immune? I shuddered to think that under different circumstances, I might have gone to him for help. Were he to find us, he might someday boast about our deaths to his friends!

If it hadn't been for those Hutus who had risked all for us- Vianney and his family, Gaetan, Gasana- I might have concluded that goodness itself is only an illusion, that the difference between a saint and a killer is little more than circumstance. It was impossible to imagine anyone from Buganza committing genocide against fellow Rwandans. It was rare there to even find any purely "Hutu" or "Tutsi" family. And yet, I was witness to Mapida's transformation into a murderer of children!

I began to earnestly pray that Mapida would not use the restroom. He would surely consider himself a hero for capturing a wanted man like me, and see to it that our deaths were as gruesome as possible.

He walked towards us, stopping near the corner of the outhouse, then pulled down the zipper of his pants, and relieved himself right by the vegetable garden! All in sight of Claude's wife, who didn't seem to find this strange in the least. From my vantage point, none of it was making any sense. I glanced towards Jeanne, who was trembling against the wall.

Mapida finished his business and walked to the entrance of the main house. Reaching up above the door, he pulled a hidden key from inside an air vent, and went in. We listened and waited. Claude's wife continued pulling vegetables, tossing them onto a wheelbarrow taken from the shed. We could hear her quiet exertions, the rhythmic *thump* of her growing harvest.

Perhaps twenty minutes later Mapida reappeared, lugging a blue basin half-filled with water. He set the basin down, removed his shirt, and started to wash his arms and chest with a bar of soap- again, in full view of the woman. It dawned on me that this fellow was showing off; a bath such as this could easily have taken place in the privacy of the outhouse.

Finishing his wash, Mapida went indoors again, emerging wearing a fresh change of clothes and holding a machete. He swept it through the air, admiring the sound it made. A wide-brimmed hat overshadowed his face. He was ready for an afternoon of murder and thievery. He said something to the woman that I could not make out, and left through the gate, as he had come.

I hated and feared the continued presence of Claude's wife in the garden, while thanking God Almighty for her at the same time. She was the reason Mapida had not used the outside restroom– never realizing as he set out to kill *inyenzi* that two of them had been hiding a meter away. It is said that God's ways are beyond understanding, and I certainly believe it. I did not know why He was keeping us alive where so many worthier men had died, but I was surely humbled because of it. As the woman finally completed her work and wheeled her harvest home, I held Jeanne's hand and we thanked Him yet again.

If Claude's wife was able to unlock the gate and gather vegetables, I thought, then Claude and Mapida both must have free reign in Nabara's home, and both of them had become bloodthirsty killers. It was certainly not safe for us to remain there another day, and only because of God's mercy and the rain had we survived this long.

It was sunny and pleasant now; all traces of the storm were gone. It was good weather for hunting cockroaches.

Chapter 6
The Midnight Voice

"If we use the word 'genocide' and are seen as doing nothing, what will be the effect on the November election?"

-Susan Rice, National Security Council, at an agency meeting, urging that the Rwandan genocide be downplayed to the public. (She was later promoted to Ambassador to the United Nations and National Security Advisor by President Barack Obama.)
April 1994

For a third day we camped inside the rickety shed, always on edge. It was April 29th– the twenty-second day since the start of that which much of the world refused to name a genocide– and late that afternoon, Nabara himself finally returned home.

If we hadn't had our encounter with his friend Mapida, we might have been willing to show ourselves, and ask him for help. But now we felt as if we could trust no one. He was alone, dressed frightfully in all black, with a wide black hat, trench coat and heavy farmer's boots.

I watched him circle the house and stroll through the back door, completely unaware that we were trespassers on his land. The familiar, sickening, quaking fear returned; the sensation of hiding under the very looming shadow of violent death. As a boy I was fond of playing hide-and-seek with my brothers and sisters; I knew the thrill of being hunted for, the tension of weighing whether to stay still or to run for it. I cannot describe the terror with which we had now grown accustomed, except to say that it was, in a perverse way, similar. We wanted to run for our lives, to scream, to close our eyes and remain cowering silently, and to throw ourselves at his feet and plead for mercy, all at once.

Nabara reemerged about an hour later with a basin full of water. It looked as if he had only returned home to wash himself, as his friend had done the day before. I wondered how far away he was staying and where he would go next. He had taken off his long outer coat, and was wearing a *mugondo*, a kind of multicolored, short-legged trousers.

We watched and waited breathlessly, as we had the day before. I could intently spy on Nabara through the tiny window of the outhouse, as he examined his face in a small handheld mirror, perhaps wondering whether to shave. His eyes were red from weeks' worth of sleepless nights.

Like his friend Mapida, Nabara came from my own hometown, a place where Hutu and Tutsi had intermarried often, and coexisted peacefully. My instincts told me that he could still be trusted. But the same had been true of Mapida, a man now consumed by hatred; our experience with Mapida gave us pause. I motioned to Jeanne, as if to ask whether I ought to appeal to Nabara for mercy and protection. She firmly motioned back in the negative. *At least not yet...*

And so we remained hidden for an hour more. It began to grow dim.

Nabara finished washing and went back inside the house to dress. I knew that in a few minutes he would probably leave, and our chance to reveal ourselves to him would be gone. The longer we hid in the outhouse, the greater the likelihood that we'd be found by Mapida or some other enemy. If we did nothing and let him depart, what would be the end for us? It was maddening to have to choose!

He came outside again, still wearing the *mugondo* and with the coat back on, carrying multiple pairs of pants. He stepped into the light to put them on, one over the other, and then sat down to tie on his boots. I looked to Jeanne again for counsel, but her head was buried in her arms. Nabara turned towards the gate, his boots falling heavily across the front lawn. I listened to the gate open and close, wondering whether my hesitation to call out was a failure of courage, or another life-saving close call. He was gone.

If he comes back within five minutes for some reason, it will be a sign that we should ask him to help us. I knew that it was foolish to think this way, especially since I was gambling with our lives, but had no time to reconsider. The gate's hinges creaked loudly once more, and Nabara reappeared on the lawn. My mind was swirling.

At the moment he passed by the outhouse, I took a deep breath and stepped out onto the path, appearing only two meters away from his shoulder, calling him by name in a low tone of voice.

He spun around and stared at me wide-eyed, as surprised as if he'd been given an electric shock.

From the inside of his coat he drew a machete.

"Nabara. Nabara," I pleaded. "Please, don't. It's me, Charles."

141

I stepped closer, afraid that he might react loudly and attract a neighbor. He didn't recognize me at first, in the dusk.

"Oh, Charles!" he gasped. I frantically motioned for him to keep his voice down, relieved that his first reaction was not to attack.

"You are still alive?" he went on. "I thought they killed you. How did you ever survive past April 7?"

Then we weren't in immediate danger, it seemed. He still held the dreaded machete in his right hand, but extended the left towards me. I shook it eagerly.

"*Pole sana kabisa ndugu yangu,*" he sighed in Swahili. "I am sorry for you, my brother. You must have suffered a lot over these last three weeks."

"Yes, brother, I suffered terribly," I plunged ahead. "That's why I thought to ask if perhaps you could hide us in your house until it is safe. We are exhausted, at the breaking point."

"We? You mean Jeanne is alive too? With "you?"

"Yes. She is in the outhouse."

He squinted in that direction, wondering at the fact that we had survived together, outlasting the slaughter. Thinking about it in hindsight, it *was* remarkable.

"Where did you stay all this time? How did you live?"

I hesitated, not wanting to compromise Gaetan. "We spend our days and nights in the bush, in the fields of sorghum and around these abandoned houses. For the last three days, we have been hiding in this toilet."

"You had remarkable luck, then. You could have been seen by anyone— especially Mapida. He comes and goes as he pleases here, any time, day or night. He is one of these murderers now. He's become really dangerous."

"Yes, that's why we were hoping to hide somewhere in your place. No one would suspect that we are there. Maybe you could find some reason to keep Mapida from coming so often. We're running out of places to go; it would save our lives."

"I'm afraid that it's impossible. If they find you here, I'm a dead man."

He opened the door of the outhouse and looked in curiously, finding Jeanne hunched fearfully against the wall. I pleaded further with Nabara, but he was adamant. We could not hide in his house, or even in the outhouse, any longer.

"Charles, you must understand how serious things have become. If we are found hiding an enemy, then we will be called traitors. My family and I would quickly be killed. It hasn't gotten any better since I left here. There are bodies piled up everywhere, too many to count. Women...children. I can't imagine it getting any worse. They killed your family and everyone in Kabeza, Charles."

"Yes," my heart sank again at this fresh mention of my brothers. "I have heard."

"Keeping you here would not save either of us." He thought for a moment. "You should try to hide at Silas' house. He has an outdoor toilet like mine. He went to his hometown in Gitarama; there's nobody there. It is dark now, you can leave right away."

He was already herding us towards the exit. "Even if you are unlucky enough to be discovered there, at least no one else will be incriminated by the Interahamwe."

It wasn't the first time we had been told that!

He escorted us through the row of eucalyptus trees at the edge of his plot of land. There was no time to ask him about any other options, or to worry about being seen this early in the evening. He was eager to part with us. As he ushered us towards the nearby home of Silas, I began to doubt whether we could really trust him. I decided to test him, as we had with young Claver.

"Nabara," I whispered, "we have not eaten for days. We don't mean to bother you, but could you leave some food with us before you go?"

"I don't know if I can find anything, but whenever I do I will come back and see you."

"Could you bring us some water, then?"

"Fine. Here we are. Wait here."

We had arrived at the tiny shed behind Silas' home. His outdoor toilet was smaller than Nabara's, and the stench even more unpleasant. Worse, there was no door; anyone passing in front of the entrance could easily spot us. Neither was Silas' property surrounded by a fence or wall, as Nabara's had been. We were exposed, and closer than before to our most feared enemies. The shacks of the displaced Hutus from Byumba and Ruhengeri in the North were adjacent to Silas' backyard. Compared to Nabara's outhouse, this was a pitiful hiding place.

Whether we were still relieved that we had survived meeting Nabara, or whether we were simply too hungry and exhausted to worry, I don't know. I only know that we curled up inside of our new, smaller outhouse home with far less trepidation than could be expected. Even Nabara, who for all we knew was rushing to bring Interahamwe thugs to surround us at that very moment, did not overly frighten us with his suspicious behavior. Indeed, he returned as promised a few minutes later with a large aluminum cup filled with water, placed it next to us, and disappeared quickly around the corner of the house. We sat and waited alone, listening for tell-tale signs that someone might have observed us during our move. None came.

It was early in the evening, and the Hutus of Kimironko were still going about their nightly business. We could watch them coming and going by the gutter behind Silas' house, to collect rainwater from tanks, barrels and jerry-cans arranged there. If one of those neighbors were to take a few steps towards the outhouse and so much as look inside, we would be ruined. The toilet was within sight and accessible to any of them, should they feel the need to use it. Jeanne surely shared my fears, but we had learned, by now, not to speak of such things. There was nothing to be accomplished by worrying.

Half an hour later, Nabara proved to be as good as his word. He came to us with an opened box of corned beef, set it down inside the outhouse, and sped away as quickly as he had come. With this food and this water, we could last for nearly three days in the tiny shed, if we were lucky enough to go unnoticed that long.

We ate some of the beef, and drank from the cup together in fear. We were huddled in the darkest and farthest corner of the tiny shed, where in the gloom we would not be seen unless someone stepped all the way inside. Only when it was pitch black did we dare to lie down, when the neighbors had all retired to their homes and the militia had presumably ceased hunting Tutsis for the night. We covered ourselves in the towels given to us by Claver, for protection against the cold and the mosquitos, clinging to one another in the dark.

Sleep did not come easily, and peace was impossible. When my mind drifted away from fears of capture, torture, and death, I found myself thinking again about my brothers, now dead, and my sisters, perhaps in terrible danger. This creeping grief and helplessness were worse than the specter of my own death– and I fought them away. It was better to stay alert, listening for any approaching footsteps or suspicious noises, than to think upon what I had lost, and go mad with sorrow and rage. I do not remember falling into a troubled sleep, but I must have, as did my wife beside me.

We both awoke to the sounds of bullets and explosions– and not in the distance. They blasted us upright. The ground shook, and our ears rang. We threw our backs against the wooden walls, speaking to one another only by frightened expression. War had come to us!

It was about ten in the morning, and the skull-splitting crack of guns seemed all around us in every direction. We thrust our fingers into our ears. Shells were crashing into roofs and walls on all sides. We could hear shouting, but it was unintelligible. The thin planks of the outhouse offered no protection at all, and we both understood that we were helpless against any stray bullet that might find us.

Until deep into the afternoon we braced ourselves, hiding as well as we could out of the line of sight of any Interahamwe or FPR soldiers that might at any moment run past, while hoping and praying against being caught in their fire. Whenever the shooting dissipated for a moment, we were left motionless, hopeful that the worst might be past, and whenever the battle drew nearer and fiercer we clenched our teeth and expected the worst. Each time Jeanne started at the sound of a particularly close blast, I feared that she had been shot through the walls, only to be reassured otherwise.

The explosions from nearby grenades devastated us the most. There was no way to prepare for them, the noise of was deafening and felt as near as the clothes on our backs. It was clear that everyone's homes, Hutu and Tutsi, were now suffering permanent damage.

If open war has come upon our neighborhood, then perhaps the rebel forces will defeat the Rwandan army and claim the area for themselves, I hoped inwardly. *If we can survive the battle, then we will be safe. But what of Gaetan and the other peace-loving Hutus who had sheltered us? Had they already fled the area? Would they be targeted together with the Interahamwe?* Not knowing what was going on was nearly as maddening as being holed up in a shed in the center of a war zone. We would be lucky to last through the day, and if we did, there was no telling what would then become of us.

Late in the afternoon, the fighting became distant, like a passing stampede. The sounds of grenades and gunfire continued, but they were farther off, as they had been intermittently throughout the last three weeks. There was no sign of FPR soldiers occupying Kimironko– only the whispers of residents cautiously emerging from their homes. The Tutsi fighters had moved the battle line elsewhere, and we were no better or worse off than we'd been yesterday.

146

Night fell, and we had survived a day filled with danger. We finished the last of the food (the water had been used up long ago), gave thanks, and slept.

The third morning passed, and still we were undiscovered. Now we were under attack from a new enemy: a sweltering heat. By early afternoon, it had become unbearable. We were dizzy with thirst, caged in and denied our share of any cool breeze by our tiny prison. Only a few meters away was the row of vessels filled with precious water. It might as well have been on the moon. We couldn't dare to approach it, exposing ourselves to the doorways and windows of our hostile neighbors. We waited for the night to come, for what seemed like years.

Jeanne grew desperate. "You can go now and quickly get some water. No one will see you in the darkness."

"I don't want to make a mistake that could cost our lives, just for a cup of water! Let's wait until at least midnight."

She agreed, but the emotional strain of the past days, coupled with the heat and thirst, began to overwhelm her. She started to sob quietly. I wanted to calm her, but decided against it; it was probably better for her to have some release. I was determined to wait as long as possible before fetching the water. I had become emotionless, at least externally; a condemned prisoner granted one stay of execution after another. I was on borrowed time, and had decided within myself to neither hope nor despair.

I had slept very little the previous two nights, and as midnight approached, I began to feel drowsy. Jeanne had herself sunk into a half-sleep. It was beautifully quiet outside; the war noises had ceased for the moment, or moved out of earshot. The only sounds were those of nature.

I heard a voice that seemed to come from nowhere in particular, addressing me by name. It frightened me at first; I wanted it to whisper instead, lest it alert our sleeping neighbors. Then I suspected that I was losing my mind. There was no one nearby to be seen. I thought I might be having an especially lucid dream, or a hallucination. I had heard of such things, but never experienced them.

To be certain, I nudged Jeanne.

"Did you say anything to me?"

"No. Why?"

"I heard someone, right here. Did you hear anything, like a voice?"

"No. What did it say?"

"It said, 'You will face great obstacles, but don't be afraid. You will not die. There is a way out and a rescue.'"

"You didn't eat or drink for a long time. It might be you imagined it."

I agreed with her. I might have. But my senses all seemed to be working faithfully, as far as I could tell. I decided not to insist, at least not to her. But I would accept this message as if it were God's own. I clung to it with all my strength, faith, and hope, and would do so for a long time to come. I had considered myself fortunate to delay death time after time, but now my confidence grew.

I said nothing to Jeanne at the moment, but knew that we were not going to die– at least not in this shed. We would soon be striking out on our own.

Chapter 7
Wits' End

"There are some groups terribly concerned about the gorillas...but– it sounds terrible– people just don't know what can be done about the people."

-Pat Schroeder, United States Congress
April 30, 1994

Early in the morning, while it was still dark, we talked over our next move. We had successfully hidden for three days, but were now deathly weak and desperate with hunger.

Jeanne confessed that she'd had enough of hiding in holes and outhouses. We whispered to one another until the sun hung high, debating over where we might go, and whether any of our other neighbors could be trusted. There didn't seem to be any new ideas.

I was certain of only one thing– we were not going to die. The terror of the previous day...we'd been sure that it was going to be our last. Now that terror was banished, by the effect of last night's mysterious voice.

Though it would only be a matter of time until we were discovered, we had no choice but to try to outlast the Interahamwe for one more day. That same night, we agreed, we would be gone from Silas' outdoor toilet. There was nowhere to run but back to Gaetan's home, despite all of the problems that would likely be caused by our reappearance at his door. We simply had no other plan. We could cling to the hope that there might be some new, positive development, since we had last left him.

For another full, agonizing day, we sat and waited for night to fall. Then we waited some more, until all was quiet. Over the course of four full days, no one had approached the outhouse of Silas for any reason. Our hunger notwithstanding, we had been fortunate here. It was an encouraging sign.

The quickest and safest way back to Gaetan's house was to retrace our steps and return the way we had come: through Nabara's property and over his fence. At 10:30 in the evening, we stole our way through the grove of trees separating Nabara's land from Silas'.

A man, framed by moonlight, was standing there.

With Jeanne behind me, I had the presence of mind to retreat around the corner of Nabara's cottage. It was Mapida.

He was drunk, and narrowly missed seeing us. We quietly waited for him to leave. Mapida's presence threatened to change all of our plans; if he was staying at Nabara's house tonight, then climbing over the nearby wall, littered as it was with broken glass, would be impossible.

So Jeanne and I patiently listened. We'd both become accustomed to a life of hiding and creeping by this point, and were no longer quite so fearful and trembling in such situations, as we'd been in the past. Mapida lumbered into the house and closed the door. He seemed intoxicated enough, we judged, that in a few minutes he'd be sound asleep, and we could attempt to scale the wall as planned.

So we waited as long as we dared, losing precious time. At last I walked across the lawn, Jeanne following. We reached the wall and stepped carefully across tiny shards of broken bottles. After peering over the wall to be sure that the area was clear, I boosted her over, as before. We took greater care this time to avoid cuts– as Jeanne sat upon the wall, I climbed over myself, and guided her down- but the darkness and the difficulty of our escape made safety impossible. I could hear her stifling cries of pain as the smallest pieces of glass on top of the fence scraped her arms and stomach.

Now between the outer wall and the road, we crouched against the earth, hiding among hibiscus flowers, resting from our stressful climb. It was still utterly dark, and still quiet, where two days before there had been a battlefield.

We were within sight of Gaetan's place, and his ruined banana plantation. With so many of the trees cut down, there would be far less cover for us. Making doubly sure that the road was clear and that no one nearby was awake, we crossed the road successfully and huddled together near our embattled friend's house. I held Jeanne's hand, and felt a trickle of blood. Feeling my way up her arm in the darkness, I discovered several bleeding cuts. She had boldly and quietly endured a difficult time. I could only hope and pray that Gaetan might be able to clean and bandage the wounds– if he was able to help us at all.

Indeed, if he even was still even living in his house! Whatever the purpose of the fighting that had overwhelmed us earlier, it might mean that Gaetan and other sensible neighbors were long gone from Kimironko, or from the city altogether.

We peered into Gaetan's bedroom window. Summoning the courage to risk capture yet again, I knocked sharply. There was no response.

In front of the main house and shop was a large shed-like structure, built to serve as an outside kitchen. The door was ajar, and we decided that we would take shelter inside for a few hours, and then try again to awaken Gaetan just before dawn.

We slipped inside the kitchen, where we were greeted by a swarm of mosquitos, taking shelter from the cold. We huddled together in the corner, covering ourselves in the towels which we still carried, hoping for a bit of rest and relief. But the cold, the insects, and especially the uncertainly of what was to come in the morning conspired to keep us awake and anxious until dawn.

The sky slowly took on its early-morning color as we sat, exhausted but with sleep still eluding us. We expected Gaetan or a member of his family to enter the kitchen at some point, at which time we could reveal ourselves to them, and ask if there was any good news or a chance of a new place to hide. We dreaded that Gaetan's dangerous cousin might still be living on the premises, and would be the first to find us, bringing ruin to all.

The first sound of a door creaking open from the house set us cowering, as far back into the kitchen's dark corner as possible, for fear of Modesto. It was Gaetan's small daughter who appeared in the kitchen doorway instead.

"Don't be afraid," I called and waved to her. "It's Charles and Jeanne." At the sound of my voice the young girl turned to see me standing upright. She was startled, but did not cry out.

"It's Charles and Jeanne. See? Jeanne is here in the corner with me. We came to hide in your kitchen."

Jeanne emerged and helped to soothe the child, caressing her hair. This helped, although my wife, in her current tattered state, must have looked more like a ghost than a family friend.

"Now please go and tell your father that we are here, and we need to talk to him."

She freed herself from Jeanne and hurried back to the house, our lives entirely in her hands. Moments later, we heard heavy footsteps approaching, and Gaetan himself joined us. Honest man that he was, his complexion had always laid his thoughts bare; his emotional state was one of disbelief, and ours a mixture of hope and shame.

"Charles, tell me, do you really want me to be killed? What are you doing, coming here again?"

I plunged ahead, sheepishly. "Gaetan, please forgive us. We know that we are creating a lot of trouble by coming back. It's just that we don't know of any other place to go. We survived for seven days and were lucky not to be found, but there is no safe place to hide, and we started to starve again. Please, have mercy on us. If there's anything you can do at all, I am sure you won't regret it."

He sighed.

"I cannot take you into my house, Charles. No one must see you."

He paused to think. "You can stay in this kitchen, but there is only one safe place in here to hide."

He pointed to a row of stacked bricks along one of the walls. "You could hide there, lying on your back, between the bricks and the wall. If you stay low to the ground, you will not be visible."

I was secretly overjoyed that he had made no mention of his cousin Modesto, which probably meant (or so I believed) that the young man was not living with Gaetan at the moment. Gaetan turned towards Jeanne, in visibly strenuous thought.

"As for you," he said at last, "We will have to take you into the house. You can fit under our bed, and pray that there won't be any searches, at least not today. Now let's hurry."

We were both tremendously relieved by Gaetan's familiar presence, his continued willingness to help us, and by the prospect of soon having something to eat. With gratitude we yielded to his plans for us.

The difficulty with my new hiding place, we found, was that I was too tall to be concealed behind the bricks. Lying on my back, I would have to bend my legs. A large desk was placed over me, and my shins pressed against it. It was extremely uncomfortable, and I wondered how long I could remain in such a torturous position.

Gaetan whispered his final instructions. "Let no one see you. Don't talk to anyone, not even my wife. No one should know that you are here. Be patient, and I will come and get you out when it is completely safe."

With that, he was gone, and Jeanne with him.

I still had taken no food or water, and was now forced to spend the entire day contorted on my back on the stone floor, my legs held above me and against the bottom of the cabinet. It quickly grew unbearable. How I fantasized about sliding out from underneath the desk and stretching! Or lying down more comfortably on my side! But space and prudence would permit neither. The most I could risk was a soft groan of misery at times, whenever I was sure no one was nearby. A girl who helped Gaetan around the shop came and prepared porridge for breakfast. I dreamt of asking her for something to eat, but could not. The same episode repeated itself at lunchtime. I imagined myself throwing off that awful desk, sitting upright, and dining and drinking, seated comfortably on the floor– but in reality I could only listen as the food was prepared in total ignorance of me.

As the afternoon came, and my body began going completely numb, I could think of nothing but Gaetan's return. I shifted my arms and legs beneath the desk endlessly while the sky gradually darkened outside.

It was about 8 o'clock when Gaetan arrived, urging me to come out quickly. With all the eagerness in the world I lurched forward to move the hated desk and rise, but couldn't. My muscles had frozen stiff. Gaetan moved the cabinet and worked to help me straighten my arms, which were locked into a bent position. I was virtually paralyzed.

Moaning in pain, I was pulled slowly to my feet. Gaetan whispered encouragements, but it was clear to him that I was in a terrible state.

"Stretch your legs," he said, "We have to walk you into the house. Modesto is going outside the annex right now, to wash his face. His back will be towards us. We have to hurry."

Modesto– then he was still living on the grounds! This gave me an even greater respect for our new friend's boldness in continuing to help us. I felt ashamed to have brought a fresh danger on his family.

As soon as I could move my legs, Gaetan hustled me out of the kitchen shed, towards the main house. My entire body was in horrible pain; I could think of little else besides seeing Jeanne safe again, resting my arms and legs, and having something to eat and drink. To realize these comforts, I would have to safely make it inside.

We walked as quickly as we dared, Gaetan propping me upright. In the evening's remaining light, I caught a glimpse of Modesto's back as we hurried those few treacherous meters between the kitchen and the front door. Gaetan kept a casual pace as we passed by, afraid to attract the attention of the young man hunched over a basin of water. He freed one hand, swung open the door, and very firmly guided me inside. We had succeeded.

It was cold in the kitchen of the house where I collapsed against the wall, far from any windows. Jeanne came, her face darkened with care over my condition. I felt as if I'd aged thirty years; I was trembling all over and in horrible pain. My shoulder blades and forearms burned and stung. Midnight voice or no, I was starting to regret having worked so hard to preserve such a meager existence: hiding in holes and outhouses from our own neighbors, eating and drinking barely enough to keep consciousness. My hope was slipping of ever seeing our children again. Only Jeanne's presence helped me to maintain composure, for her sake– and the despair was manifest in her as well.

The kitchen grew hot and filled of smoke from the firewood used for cooking. Gaetan's family brought me precious food and water, but there was an uncomfortable silence between us all. It was really too much for them to continue to shelter "Tutsi cockroaches" like us, with the risk increasing every day. We knew this, and our minds and theirs were busy with the unspoken question: What would be done about us?

Neither of our party dared to utter a word. It was Gaetan who finally sighed and broke the silence.

"Charles, we are planning to close up the house and flee the area."

"You are running away? From whom? I don't understand."

"The situation has become impossible. Did you hear the fighting going on two days ago? Perhaps wherever you were hiding, you did not see it."

Jeanne and I exchanged looks.

"The FPR came. They chased the FAR out of many of their positions in Kigali. The FAR fought them off here, but they might come back. Our neighborhood is becoming a battleground!"

"If the FPR take Kimironko," I offered, "it would be good news for Jeanne and I."

"And very bad news for us. This massacre is being talked about all over the world– they think that over half a million people were killed already. UNAMIR is mostly gone;

they won't come to restore peace. What if the rebels win this war? The FPR won't know who was a killer and who wasn't, and they likely won't care. They could take revenge on every Hutu. How could I prove that I wasn't one of these Interahamwe?"

It struck me for the first time that Gaetan's situation and mine could easily be reversed soon.

"Besides," he went on, "if you try to hide here, you will almost certainly be shot by the FAR before any rebels could come rescue you. These are not just thugs with machetes, Charles. The FAR coming in force to Kimironko would be far worse than what you have already dealt with. You have made a tunnel inside of that hole outside. I suggest you hide there, and extend it as much as you can. There is no better hiding place. God willing, you can survive until the FPR take Kimironko and the fighting is over. Then maybe you can show yourself to them, and be safe."

My heart fell at the very mention of that dreaded hole! Not even for one night would I return to that awful place! Jeanne's terrified expression said the same.

"No, Gaetan, there is no way we can return to that pit."

"You must listen to reason, Charles, and be strong until the end. It's your only chance. If we are gone, then we cannot be incriminated if you're found there. Trust me; if the Hutu still hold on to this area, I will come back from time to time to check on the house, and I will bring you food, as long as I am still alive."

I protested again. "Could we not hide in this house?"

"Impossible. You know that the FAR can come into any house. You would be found immediately. I know that the hole is unpleasant, but if they can't see you in the secret cave of yours, then you might have a chance. There is no safe place anymore– not anywhere on this side of the battle-lines..."

I entreated Gaetan a few more times to find another way, but there was no escaping that we couldn't suggest a better plan than his. I dreaded the thought of descending back down into the hole; Jeanne was near tears. I felt sick to my stomach. Nevertheless, I gave up and agreed to return there, in the hope that the FPR might prove victorious soon.

It was decided that I would go alone into the pit first, and expand the secret cave as much as I could. The following night, Jeanne would be brought in, just as had been done the first time, what seemed like ages ago. I did my best to comfort Jeanne, reminding her that we had to consider the safety of Gaetan's family, and suggesting to her that the FPR might occupy all of Kigali in just a few days. We could then leave the city and go to Kenya, to our children! I myself scarcely believed it, but the memory of the midnight voice gave me strength. I resigned myself to dwell in the darkness, one last time. If the voice was truly God's and could be trusted, then I could believe that our salvation would arrive before we starved or were caught inside of that pit.

For twenty more minutes, I was allowed to rest and regain some of my strength. I assured Jeanne, somewhat dishonestly, that I was strong enough to go and dig. There were no other people on whom to rely. Gaetan and his family were our only remaining allies, and now they were preparing to flee! I was left clinging to the companionship of nocturnal voices, which, in more peaceful times, might have seemed insane.

Gaetan prepared to rush me through the banana plantation once again. We waited by the door, with the lamp out. He seemed lost in thought.

I wondered whether I would ever see him again. This family had risked their lives needlessly for our sake. They were in danger from Hutu and Tutsi alike. It was hard to see how they could ever enjoy a normal life again here in Kigali. They were not cockroaches, nor were they killers, but the events of the past month had ruined them all the same.

We waited on in silence together, standing side by side at the doorway. The door was only cracked open, and Gaetan was peering thoughtfully outside. He was waiting for the ideal moment to hurry us both out, but seemed lost and distracted, as if the chirping of crickets had sent his mind elsewhere. I wanted to seize on that quiet moment, to speak some comfort to him…to thank him.

"Gaetan...whatever happened to your brother, Fidele? Is he alive?" I felt bold enough now to risk asking.

"I trust that he is," he continued staring directly ahead, in a dream. "He was able to escape Kimironko during the fighting, through the battle lines, and enlist in the FPR. Perhaps you may meet him someday soon, if you are fortunate enough. You might tell him that we are well."

"I hope to. And if God gives me such a privilege, I will do all I can to let everyone know that you are a hero to the Tutsi...not a killer."

A moment later we were stealthily working our way towards the place I'd sworn never in my life to return.

I wasted no time and commenced digging. The work was slower than before, as my body was sore, and near the breaking point. I pushed myself onward by the recollection of the midnight voice. I remembered it as clearly as if it were still ringing in my ears. It seemed to me to have been the voice of the One who had protected us, for some purpose, until now. The voice of God.

The dust collected in my mouth. My lungs, nose, and mouth became cold metal. I was having difficulty breathing. I spat frequently and blew my nose; mucus mixed with dust collected on my face and clothes. I had scarcely slept for days.

Dawn broke overhead, and I was compelled to dig more quietly. Birds were singing, and I could see the fruits of my labor by the early morning sun: I had carved out enough space for both of us to hide more comfortably than before.

My legs could hardly bend, and it was with some difficulty that I laid myself down in the tiny fissure, to sleep at last.

I thought about the assault on our home, the morning after the assassination. I remembered running from the soldiers and Interahamwe, hiding with Dr. Alphonse Biramvu, appealing to Gaetan by faith, and spending eighteen days in this very hole, hunted by the militia above.

And now we are back again. And Gaetan will not even be in the city...

I thought, as I often had these weeks, about my children, safe in Kenya. Perhaps by now they had already mourned for us, believing us dead. I felt the warm nostalgia of a hundred beautiful memories with them. Lyndz, Yves, Luke...if I could only see them for a moment, I would die peacefully, and willingly!

I thought about the God of my youth, and the joy I had known when I first trusted in him. I had gained all I'd ever wanted in Kigali– wealth, a home, a family– but I had forgotten Christ. Now Christ was all we had left to cling to. All else had been lost. Our house, car, and belongings mattered very little now. Even my life– how carefully I had preserved it for so many years, not realizing how quickly it could be taken away! Still, I wanted more than ever to survive now, if only to share what I had learned with my children. I prayed silently, as I had weeks ago, from this very place. In the valley of the shadow of death, indeed.

I was aware of His calming presence once more, like a familiar friend now, rather than the fearsome deity I'd approached so shamefully weeks before in desperation. I passed into the sleep of a dead man, still lost in the peace of that silent time of prayer.

I slept continuously until early in the evening, when I was awakened by Gaetan's voice, whispering excitedly down to me. He had come earlier than expected, and without Jeanne. There must have been a change of plans, then. We might not be moving back into our subterranean apartments after all.

As quickly as I could, I loosened up my limbs and made the agonizing slow climb to the surface. I was filled with hope. Gaetan must have found a better hiding place! The fact that I might have spent an entire night digging for no reason bothered me not in the least. It was worth it to be truly free of the place!

Goodbye, blessed, cursed hole, I thought as I quietly staggered behind Gaetan, back towards the house. It was curious, I thought, that he would risk being seen this early in the evening.

Back inside, Dianne offered me a cup of hot tea, which felt like an elixir of life. I could hardly refrain from asking her for another one. Jeanne came and sat next to me, and we waited hopefully for whatever fresh news our benefactors had for us.

Gaetan had left us in the kitchen for a moment, but soon returned with a pained expression, and a dirty sheet of paper in his trembling hand. He invited me to come and read it. The note had been sent to him by Modesto, he said, and my own heart stopped for fear before I had read a dozen words:

Gaetan,
I know that you have Charles and his wife hidden in the pit behind your house. Everyone is whispering about it. They all suspect you of helping them. I ask you to please think about your wife and children. Drive those two out from your place right now. They are going to come and raid your house when you least expect it, and there had better not be any Tutsis there. You know what will happen to you if there are.

So then, it was no secret that we were here. The only next step for them was to come and cut us to pieces, along with Gaetan and everyone else. Modesto, it appeared, was offering Gaetan a chance to appear innocent of sheltering *inyenzi;* an only chance, which he would certainly have to take. We couldn't spend another moment beneath his roof.

Gaetan collapsed onto his living room couch, head in hands. He seemed to be straining for an idea that might save us all, to no avail. He shook his head.

"The only safe place is with the FPR itself. You'll just have to try to get to the National Stadium," he offered meekly.

"The Stadium? Why?"

"The rebels have occupied it, and some of the last remaining United Nations soldiers. That's where you would have to go to be safe. The roads there are all blocked and guarded day and night by the Interahamwe, but there is no other choice. You'll just have to try to get through them."

I seized upon this last hope. "Do you think we have any chance of reaching it? Even one in a thousand?"

"Fidele did, but that was during the battle. It's possible. With both of you together, it will be much harder. But there's no other place to go. The National Stadium of Remera is the only refuge now for someone like you."

Until now we had survived by keeping within Kimironko, staying away from roads and encampments of the militiamen by hiding close to home. We had dreaded taking the suicide leap of trying to travel past the roads. Now we would have to embrace it.

"We shall leave at once. What's the best way there from here?"

Gaetan explained that there were two possible routes to the stadium, both of which required us to march directly through the assembled forces of the FAR and the Interahamwe. One path required us to pass by several of their road blocks, and also to somehow creep, undetected, across wide open fields before reaching the stadium. The second route involved fewer militia checkpoints, but our path would skirt the local headquarters of the Interahamwe, at an old marketplace for used goods. It was near a dangerous paved road that would be well-traveled by the FAR.

We decided to risk the hornets' nest that was the Interahamwe headquarters, and take the second route.

"There is a fence beyond the road," Gaetan mused. "Perhaps, God willing, you can get to it; it's along the border of the IAMSEA Institute. If you make it there unseen, you can blend in with the maize and sorghum fields there, and get closer to the stadium with some cover."

"Thank you, brother. We are sorry to have brought this trouble to you. We can hide in the shadows outside somewhere until midnight, and then begin."

"No, you should travel right now instead. The militias are more distracted before midnight; many of them go out to the bars or walk around on business. At twelve-o'clock the night-watch shift will start, and the roadblocks will be more vigilantly guarded. You should try to get as far as you can before then."

Gaetan's advice was good. I looked to Jeanne, visibly shaking with the fear of a novice soldier minutes away from her first battle. *If I was traveling alone, I could crawl and snake my way through the shadows. Can my poor Jeanne possibly go on her stomach all the way from here to the National Stadium? She is already badly cut and bruised. There is no way we can go upright and on foot, unnoticed...*

Our way to the stadium was across a kilometer of brush, thorns, and stones. I winced at the mere thought of the suffering that I was inflicting upon my unhappy wife! And yet I could find no way to spare her, either. We could die here in Kimironko, or else die trying to reach the stadium. I would have to protect Jeanne as best I could, and we would either live or die together.

I looked to Gaetan. "Do you have anything black for my wife to wear? With these clothes on she'll be too conspicuous." Besides the bright colors, Jeanne's clothing was also covered in splinters and briars. She had worn the same jeans since the beginning of the genocide. I thought that she could at least have more comfortable garments for her journey.

Gaetan and Dianne hurried into the bedroom, returning with a dark red shirt. Gaetan offered the black jogging pants that he himself had been wearing. While Jeanne changed, I asked for some water in a basin with which to soak my own clothes, loosening the dried mud caked on my shirt and pants. They had become like cardboard, and would have been noisy to crawl around in, if left dry.

Our path, then, would take us through the barriers and checkpoints erected by the Rwandan Armed Forces, guarded by their soldiers and the Interahamwe's hired killers.

If we could navigate our way past them unseen, we'd then be forced to crawl through the blighted fields of sorghum and corn along the Institute's fence. The danger we faced, in making that crawl, was not only from the chance of discovery by soldiers, but also from packs of feral dogs known to roam the area. Since hundreds of human bodies had been tossed into those fields, the wild beasts had developed a hunger for human flesh, and grown bold enough to attack passersby as well.

We agreed to set out on our final journey at eight o' clock. In the past, it had been wise to wait until late in the evening before traveling outside, but on this venture, Gaetan reminded us, we would be passing by the Interahamwe guards regardless. Better to move about in the hour when they were least alert.

It was an emotional time, waiting for the 8 o'clock hour to strike, but I was without feeling, or fear. We had done all that we could to ready ourselves for this last lunge towards freedom, and whatever fate awaited us was entirely up to the Creator. It was a paradox of the human psyche that one could grow more serene while drawing nearer to death! Perhaps whatever reserves of terror, sorrow, or rage I had possessed were now spent. There was nothing left but to wait, and to think.

It occurred to me to ask Gaetan for a pencil and paper. I hurriedly scribbled a phone number and address on it

"Our children are in Nairobi with their uncle. Here is the address..." I reduced my voice to a whisper. "If you see our bodies, or hear that we were caught, please let him know. He will take care of them..."

Gaetan wordlessly took the scrap of paper from me. It was 8 o'clock.

Gaetan's entire household had now met together in the darkened living room, to see us for the last time. I gathered them all for one final prayer, beginning by thanking the Father for our host family, and for their sacrifices and kindness towards us.

"Without them," I prayed, fighting to keep the mastery of my voice and to fight back tears, "we would never have survived this long. They are Hutu, but they did all they could for us. Please keep them from harm, and us...so that perhaps we can meet again in safety. Really, Lord, we now know what real brotherhood and friendship are because of them. There are no words..."

I was unable to continue. Gaetan and Dianne offered their own prayers. We embraced their family, down to the youngest daughter, and drew near to the door.

"Cross the street in front of the market," Gaetan instructed, motioning with his hands, "and enter the unfinished house there. It will give you some cover up until the intersection on the right side. You'll have to pass the roadblock there, and a couple of others, so stay down until you reach the junction that turns towards the IAMSEA. God be with you, brother."

"You too, brother."

He opened the door.

We silently stepped outside, into the shadows around the house. Our last glimpse of the two came as they shut the door. Not an ordinary man and woman!

I was unafraid for the moment. All of my energy funneled into a singular determination to reach the stadium, with Jeanne, at all costs. There was a sense of finality to all of this. Whether we lived or died, our troubles were coming to an end.

The National Stadium, as it was.

The National Stadium, after a recent renovation.

Chapter 8
Three Hundred Meters

Genocide Investigation: Language that calls for an international investigation of human rights abuses and possible violations of the genocide convention. Be Careful. Legal at State was worried about this yesterday– Genocide finding could commit [America] to actually "do something."

-Internal letter from the office of the U.S. Secretary of Defense
May 1, 1994

We knelt alone in the bush, left to ourselves. From henceforth there would be no more hunting for hiding places, hoping to outlast and outlive the neighbors who had corrupted themselves into seething, avaricious enemies. We were in full flight for the National Stadium.

Each window of every sinister, battered house and shanty seemed as if it were watching us as we darted from shadow to shadow in the direction of the road. It was early in the evening, and we could hear families conversing; children shouting in play. Every fresh sound sent our hearts leaping into our throats. Our only supplies were our jackets and the denim pants that Jeanne had worn for weeks on end, now replaced by cotton sweats of Gaetan's. I carried them in my hands, wrapped in one of the old loincloths. Now we were crouched in the shrubbery along the side of the open road, meters away from the nearest house, in the company of crawling and buzzing insects.

"First we must be as careful as possible crossing this road," I whispered into Jeanne's ear. "Maybe–

She squeezed my hand.

"Look. Two people are coming on the street."

From thirty meters to our left, a couple was walking down the road towards us. We flattened ourselves against the ground, the bushes giving us ample protection.

For ten minutes we cringed there among the undergrowth. The pair passed by us, but from our vantage point we could see the comings and goings of others as well, both on and near the street. More than half of them appeared drunk. Some stumbled by the road, others were propped up by spouses, or more likely, prostitutes. It seemed as if a new traveler or couple would appear just as soon as the former was out of sight. The street, I thought, would never be clear.

I whispered my musings to Jeanne. "You see that most of these people are drunk, walking with prostitutes or Tutsis whom they have enslaved. I think we could get across by pretending to be like them. Shouldn't be too hard."

I was secretly pessimistic about our chances. In truth, I felt as if we were more likely to die than to even reach the first roadblock.

She silently nodded.

"I will cross the street, swerving like a drunkard," I said. "Watch me, and then do as I do and join me."

We waited until no one was immediately nearby. Suppressing my fears and pulling myself to my feet by sheer willpower, I staggered into plain sight in the street.

There was a lone man gaily humming as he strolled towards me, a machete swinging in his right hand. He was thankfully drunk, and my terror failed to register with him as I turned my face away quickly, to hide my Tutsi features. He said something friendly and incoherent to me as he passed. I mumbled back, playing as best I could the part of a carefree, inebriated townsperson. And so we passed by one another peacefully; two cordial drunkards on their way home.

I purposefully faltered as I neared the opposite side of the road, doubling over in some tall grass. Staying stooped down, I lurched and zigzagged, making steady progress towards the nearby field, where some distance away stood the unfinished skeleton of a house which Gaetan had given to us as a marker for our journey. Past the road and in shadow, I turned and looked anxiously back for Jeanne

She had already begun to cross, haltingly, as I had, playing the part well. But fear was overtaking her performance.

A man and woman were visible some distance away, coming straight towards Jeanne. Appearing to panic, she broke into a run. I could only watch powerlessly, weighing how to best intervene if the advancing couple raised the alarm. Instead, I watched Jeanne expertly fall to the ground over her own feet, landing onto her knees in the center of the street. She gathered herself awkwardly and half-walked, half-fell, rather quickly, collapsing again into a heap in the tall grass. Her back now safely turned to the approaching pair, they regarded her with amusement, and she limped to my hiding place, quickening her pace once the threat had passed by.

I had watched the entire scene unfold under the moonlight, petrified. Now I embraced Jeanne, grinning, as she met me in the brush.

"You were fantastic!" I congratulated her, whispering into her ear. "I thought that you were going to panic, but your performance was masterful. You are a great actress."

She scowled.

"I am not. I tripped trying to run."

I meekly offered something to the effect of "all's well that ends well," but I was only talking with myself. Jeanne had already turned to survey the field ahead.

I joined her at the corner of the field, within view of the skeletal house. We both remembered Gaetan's advice on how best to navigate the way towards the checkpoint.

"We both have to crawl on our bellies from now on, Charles." My wife was more determined than I had ever seen her. "You lead the way, and try to move any sharp objects you find. I will follow directly behind, and do my best not to moan or express any pain."

She was referring to the still-burning cuts and bruises across her arms and stomach. Gaetan's wife had made some effort to clean and dress them, but Jeanne's journey was about to become torturous, even so. I was taken by her stoicism in the face of pain and the threat of danger. She had certainly changed over the past month.

The unfinished house loomed only about ten meters ahead and to our right, a hulking black spider's web of lumber rising up into the moonlight. Below, and all around, was only a sea of black. As planned, we launched out on our stomachs into that darkness, slithering forwards and gaining only inches at a time, looking up to the house occasionally to get our bearings. I was parting the tall grass with my hands, feeling for stones and whatever else I could move aside. After two meters and only a few minutes into our crawl, we were visited by a fresh new horror– one that violently hit our nostrils, and moments later our eyes.

The awful stench was that of decaying bodies. It grew stronger with every inch we progressed, until the grass before us gave way to the first of hundreds of them.

Rotten, wasted corpses were strewn about in front of us. They were scattered all across the field, attended by buzzing flies and worms. We had heard dogs barking in the distance since earlier that evening; now we could hear them growling and snapping at one another ahead. They were feasting on human flesh.

Neither of us could move forward another inch. My stomach lurched and I turned my head and vomited, revulsion and nausea mingled with new fear. We had crawled directly into our worst nightmare.

I took hold of Jeanne's trembling hand. She was struggling against her every impulse not to scream or weep.

She buried her head beneath her arms, stifling the sobs, hiding her nostrils from the air filled with the decay of our neighbors.

But she did not move backwards, either– not in the slightest. Though no words were exchanged between us, we both knew that there was no other path but the hellish one directly before us.

The half-built house was only a stone's throw away. Had we been able to stand and make a run for it, we would have reached it the place a matter of seconds. And how we longed to! Forced instead to creep over and through our fellow Rwandans' corpses, we could think of nothing else but gaining that house and leaving the field of horrors behind us forever.   Crawling as we were, surrounded everywhere by watchful eyes, our survival depending upon stealth...we could only inch our way along, at eye-level with rotting and soft limbs, bodies...faces. A journey that should have taken twenty seconds lasted more than twenty minutes, and seemed like twenty lifetimes.

As often as we could, we held our eyes closed, opening them only as much as necessary to navigate towards the house and across the human debris. I held my breath for minutes at a time; with every inhalation my chest and stomach heaved. By our elbows we dragged ourselves, dreading to let our eyes wander. Jeanne followed my feet as they slid along the blood-stained grass, and I, leading the way, tried my best to make her path bearable, jostling aside heads and limbs with my shoulders. I could do little without drawing attention to our movements. I feared that something might startle my wife; her nerves had already been tested beyond reason. If she were to see a particularly gruesome, disfigured face...or worse yet, to come across a body which we recognized...it was better not to imagine the worst, only to crawl onwards in a miserable, feverish dream.

For compassion's sake I will spare you from the worst details of our journey through that cursed field. What hell, prepared for the devil and his angels, could match the torture of the evils created by man in times such as these?

It's likely for the best that we could not be aware of the lengths being taken, at that very moment, by the world's superpowers to vehemently deny that "genocide" was even occurring. As we labored to cling to life, surrounded by the systematically murdered bodies of Tutsi men, women, and children, the American State Department and its U.N. allies were collaborating to shirk their duties to the United Nation's genocide convention. What was happening to us was a "conflict", there was "unrest"; perhaps some "atrocities" had been committed. But politicians and their spokespersons hedged and grew disingenuous when asked if there was, in fact, a "genocide" taking place in tiny Rwanda.

Of course, the reality of genocide was never in doubt. The peacekeepers had witnessed the massacres for themselves. Government radio broadcasts in Rwanda publicly called for the extermination of all Tutsi. President Habyarimana, prior to his death, had overseen the development of the Interahamwe himself– his own private killing force. Their stockpiling of explosive weapons, guns and machetes was no secret either; U.N. member nations themselves had supplied much of the weaponry and training for the eventual killers. Aid workers were reporting that the Interahamwe were bent on killing the future generation of Tutsi as well, by methodically murdering pregnant women and children. Hundreds of thousands were dying. By every possible definition– and by every single one of the criteria named in the revered U.N. genocide charter– Rwanda was experiencing genocide.

The awful truth would have only crushed our spirits further had we understood it then: Rwanda was simply not worth it to the Europeans, to the Americans…to the world at large. Decades ago they had pledged together to "never again" tolerate genocide; now the smallest of sacrifices was considered too great, even the cost of keeping the few-hundred UNAMIR soldiers in place. They chose to dishonor their decades-old pact; to mutually look the other way from the face of evil. And evil feasted.

Jeanne and I did overcome, or rather survive, the trek through that open mass grave. The feral dogs, who were never seen but whose bone-chilling cries seemed to come from everywhere, seemed content to gnaw on the dead rather than to pursue living food.

We dragged ourselves across the concrete foundation of the unfinished house, staying in the shadow of a patch of finished wall. Jeanne shook and sobbed; my skin crawled and writhed against the cold stone, as though I could scrape the stench of the field from my body. I don't know how long we lied there, gasping for clean air and convulsing, unable to scream or weep. Ahead of us now was a row of occupied houses, and in that direction, away from the awful field behind, our eyes stayed fixed.

Within the house directly ahead, closest to us, a light glowed, and on the lawn there were men loitering, perfectly at ease. I positioned myself as near as possible to them while keeping to the shadows, hoping to hear snatches of their conversation. To my shock, I saw that these were not mere citizens, but commandos from the military camp of Kanombe who had set up in Kimironko and requisitioned that house, transforming it into their barracks.

The next street over, which merged into the road leading away to the IAMSEA, was on the other side of this house, and past the roadblock there was the junction that would take us on to the National Stadium. We would first have to creep our way alongside this house, and then the next– in the very shadow of the barracks of FAR soldiers. It was an unexpected new problem.

Beyond the houses, I could see the main road. We would be required to creep past our enemies along the wall of the barracks house, and then somehow race into the shadow of the house beyond. From there, it was a sharp right turn– with no cover at all– to the main street, which we would attempt to cross. After that there would be barriers, erected by the militia and soldiers, well-guarded. This was the route recommended to us by Gaetan, and I was ready to hold to it, though the militia roadblocks weighed heavily on my mind. I could not imagine a way around or through them.

For a few minutes more we rested and renewed our courage. I watched the soldiers– they were eating dinner now, both inside and outside of their commandeered quarters. They were as cheerful as you could imagine; seeming not the least bit at war. There was the occasional joke and accompanying burst of laughter. More of them poured out of the house, and then back in again, a handful always remaining to chat away in the warm night air. It seemed that getting along the wall of that house, and passing safely by it, would be impossible.

There was no route by which we could avoid their notice, I thought.

On the other hand, if we choose to deviate a bit from Gaetan's instructions, we can avoid this house, and cross the road to our right instead. Then we can circle back to the originally planned path at the intersection...

It was a detour that gave us an extra Interahamwe roadblock or two to cross, with enemies no doubt walking about between the barriers as well. Gaetan had sent us on what he thought was the path with the fewest dangers, but surely he had expected this row of houses to be occupied only by sleeping neighbors, and not a troop of trained killers! It might be better to take our chances with a threat not yet seen, rather than one that was clearly an impossible situation.

Jeanne was, with me, now intently watching the uniformed men idling about the house. Their weapons were more deadly than those of the Interahamwe, and they were better trained in the use of them. I decided that we would not, and could not, choose to go directly into their hands. We would take our chances with the roadblocks and the militiamen instead. I whispered as much to Jeanne, and she nodded. There was a special kind of serenity that I observed in her, as I explained how we would draw away from the barracks-house, back and to the side, crossing the road to the right out of their view, giving a wide berth to their quarters.

We would have to walk briskly and naturally, as quietly as possible, hoping not to attract a closer look in case we were seen.

One last time I reflected on the congregation of soldiers, and noted their comings and goings. Some were heading off somewhere, or traveling from house to house. One pair argued about something just out of my hearing. Nearly all were jubilant– energized by a time of relaxation after a day of massacres, well-rewarded for their efforts with hemp and alcohol, soldiers and citizen militia alike.

Such a disgrace upon beautiful Rwanda, I thought. They celebrated only meters away from the dumping grounds of the bodies of thousands of neighbors, mothers, fathers, and children whom they had only just killed. It was an impossible thing to fathom. Clearly the world was filled with thieves, with neither fear of God nor conscience, willing to take advantage of the ignorant and desperate, inflaming their worst passions in the name of liberty.

Although we were going to forego heading directly towards the FAR troops, we would still need to find the way across the road that afforded us the best chance at secrecy. We left our secure hiding place and shuffled towards the street to our right, staying beneath the bush. There was plenty of brush by the curb, and we scuttled on our stomachs, flush with the ground. The militia's headquarters were somewhere ahead of us, and we would have to choose a crossing-point with it somewhere to our right, and the soldiers' barracks to our left.

For nearly thirty minutes we waited, as I strained my eyes in every direction, watching the people come and go, contemplating the best method by which to cross.

We cannot be this afraid to cross every street...we are waiting too long, making too little progress. There will be at least two roads to cross more dangerous than this one, with guarded roadblocks...if we continue at this slow pace, the sun will rise on us before we get to the stadium...

I was surprised, after about half an hour of uncertain watching, to see fewer and fewer men walking about. I wondered if the soldiers were expected to take their supper at a particular time. Was it happening now?

Several times I nearly bolted for the road, only to check myself. There were just a few people nearby, and we remembered Gaetan's warning that the patrols grew more vigilant late at night.

There might never be a better moment to cross if we don't do it now...

Once again we would play the part of a drunkard and his Tutsi prize, a "prostitute cockroach" as they were called.

We would surely be seen by someone, but as long as we were not approached up close and did not attract any special attention, it might not matter. I resolved to cross at the next possible moment.

"Jeanne," I whispered, "it's now or never. You see over there, where there is a light and men standing around? The Interahamwe roadblock is over there. We will cross this road and then get as close as we can to the roadblock before lying down and crawling again. There are some houses there...we will try to lie down next to one. From there we will decide what to do next. Come, we'll cross together this time."

We swallowed our fears and stood. That first moment, as we rose out of the brush, was for me the most frightening. A man and woman crossing the street might not merit any closer investigation– but a couple springing up out of the bushes–! It would be fatal to have been watched in that instant, though we didn't have the luxury of looking around to see if we'd been noticed. Clinging to one another, we stepped into the middle of the road.

Our fearful trembling must have aided us in our impersonation of a drunken man and his horrified captive. Out of the corner of my eye I could see the dark expanse of the field, hiding the piles of corpses, behind me and to the right. How many murders had occurred lately along this very road! My legs were more wobbly than I had expected them to be, and my wife's trembled and shook as well. For too long we had crawled, crouched, and hidden along the ground. Walking upright was now surprisingly trying.

As planned, we reached the opposite curb, hope increasing with every second that passed without a voice hailing us, or footsteps in pursuit.

We strolled and stumbled into the shadows of trees and houses, wincing at every snapped twig or crushed leaf, resisting the urge to break into a run towards our ultimate goal– the farthest house in the clearing.

It was a small dwelling, outside of a circle of homes, its front door directly before us. We walked towards its right side, intending to crouch down in the shadows there, creep around to the rear of the house, and rest a moment with a good view of the roadblock. Instead, as we were only ten steps from the door, it opened.

A man descended the two front steps, and looked directly at us. In our surprise, we had no time to react in any way, but he turned away to his right– our left– paying us no mind. He had come outside to relieve himself at the side of the house.

After overcoming the initial shock of this without betraying ourselves, we could only continue walking in a straight line, passing by the house, while the stranger went about his business. It would not do to hide against the wall now, nor could we even stop walking without arousing suspicion. He would have to believe that we were heading towards some destination beyond him, or else all was lost. And yet we were striding towards the road and the Interahamwe checkpoint, and greater danger.

I slowed our pace, praying mentally that he would think nothing of us. We could distinctly see the barrier blocking the next road, and the blurry shapes of colorfully-dressed men with machetes standing nearby, in the glow of a small fire. We couldn't dare to walk any closer...

The door to the house behind us opened and closed again, now some distance behind us. We dropped to the ground behind a pair of trees, nearer to our enemies than I had intended. But we were safe enough here, hiding in the bush, as long as we stayed quiet.

The familiar smell of rotted flesh returned to our nostrils. As we settled down in silence, the sounds of flies came into focus as well, sometimes buzzing about our ears.

There must be even more bodies tossed nearby. Tutsis who had tried to escape along the road, perhaps...

Eyes adjusting once again to the darkness, we took our bearings. We were close to the road; if we raised ourselves only a few inches above the brush, we could see it.

It curved around us, and directly ahead was the Interahamwe checkpoint– a barrier built from chopped-down tree trunks, just out of reach of the fire's light. The road continued on towards the IAMSEA Institute, and far beyond that, the National Stadium.

We could also now see that the few remaining trees nearby supported dead bodies, tossed upon their roots, all around the checkpoint. We could vaguely make out some of the slumped, distorted human shapes. They had been killed, most likely by the very blades and guns clasped by the men not thirty meters away. Once again a crippling fear rose up within us and took hold. Nothing could push us any closer to that horrible roadblock– and yet our only path to freedom lay beyond it, in the fields of corn and sorghum on the other side of the IAMSEA fence. Our hope failed us.

We breathed more heavily, as if gasping for courage. I thought it might help to talk over our plans.

"It's still pretty early in the evening," I whispered directly into Jeanne's ear. "We can wait and see if they will start to slack off..." I decided to lay out a best-case scenario as if it were likely to happen. "They might leave the barrier vacant for a while, and give themselves a break...we would only need a minute to get across the road."

Our eyes stayed fixed on the barricade. We waited.

Directly behind the makeshift fence were the unmoving shapes of what looked to be two guards, seated on the ground. Some distance away was the larger body of patrolmen, having a conversation. They had built a fire and stood in a circle round it, laughing and talking. The sitting guards posed the greater threat, as the safest way to cross the road was by crawling behind the barrier itself, using it for shelter. To do so would, if we were quiet, prevent the standing group of Interahamwe from seeing us– but bring us right past the very feet of the two seated in silent vigil in the dark.

For several minutes, there was not a hint of movement by the barricade. The two guards sat as still as stones. It puzzled us both.

"What do you think about this?" I knew that Jeanne was wondering at the same thing.

"I don't know for sure. It makes no sense. They haven't moved at all. Maybe they passed out drunk. It's impossible to tell in the darkness."

For thirty more minutes we watched and waited; still the men by the fire joked and talked, and the seated Interahamwe did not move. I leaned into the ear of Jeanne again.

"I am going to look closer. If I stay completely down by the ground, I can hide on the opposite side of the barrier where they won't see me."

She clutched my arm. I went on whispering confidently in her ear.

"If I see that it's safe and those men are fast asleep, then I will continue on past the blockade. If you see me cross, then make sure that the way is safe, and follow me quickly towards the cornfield. We have to try it." I didn't bother to lay out a possible course of action to take in case I was seen and caught. There was none.

I demonstrated to her how I was going to crawl flat along the ground, slithering like a reptile onto the road on the far side of the barricade. Only by keeping close against the wooden beams could we stay out of the field of vision of the nearby guards, crawling, as it were, right underneath their noses. The sounds I was sure to make– however carefully I crossed– would prove fatal if either of the sitting men were awake and alert.

"Staying flat against the ground like this is the only way to succeed. Please be careful." There was pleading in her eyes, and so I added, "I will be back with you soon, hopefully on the other side. Don't worry, love."

182

I started my creep along the ground toward the barrier, peering towards the two motionless guards with every few inches of progress. Nothing changed. The roadblock extended almost into the brush along the side of the road, and so my cover, though not ideal, was satisfactory enough that I was emboldened to continue my progress until my face was near the barrier itself. Once I passed behind it, I wouldn't be able to glance towards the guards until I had reached the opposite side.

The standing, chatting group of militiamen was still a safe distance away. I could hear snatches of their idle conversation now. I took one final look towards the unmoving, sitting silhouettes of the guards near the barricades, and my heart leapt for joy as my eyes adjusted and could finally make out their features. They were not men at all– only plastic racks of beer bottles left behind the barricade, perhaps to be used as stools. The Interahamwe had left their post completely unguarded!

Newly inspired by our incredible good fortune, I shimmied behind the barricade more quickly, taking a thousand precautions not to be seen or heard by the men chatting in the distance. I gently moved the smallest twigs and stones away from my path, clearing a safer trail for myself and Jeanne. When at last I could extend my head past the opposite side of the log wall, I strained my eyes again in the direction of the circle of Interahamwe. They still talked, still neglectfully far from the so-called cockroach scuttling away and out of their grasp! I slipped into the brush, completely free of the road, swallowed up once again by the safety of tall bushes. Less than fifty yards away were a combination of hired killers and trained fighters, completely lacking in any vigilance, perhaps convinced that there wasn't a single surviving Tutsi left to try to flee through their trap!

I settled in to see whether Jeanne would also safely cross. Bravely she emerged from the brush, sliding along at a maddeningly deliberate pace, stopping frequently.

It was a more painful journey for her; forced as she was to drag her torn, wounded body against the dust and the cold street. As she passed completely behind the barricade, she rested more frequently and for longer periods, frozen by either pain or fear.

If anything is going to be our undoing, it is Jeanne's poor condition, I fretted. *It won't be easy for her to survive the rest of the way...*

Gathering herself, she made a final, careful lunge towards the bushes, arriving safely next to me. She had seen for herself that the roadblock was unguarded, and taken new courage.

The time, I guessed, was about ten o'clock in the evening. We'd left Gaetan's only two hours ago, and had advanced little more than three hundred meters. After crawling to put some distance between ourselves and the treacherous checkpoint, we huddled together for a few minutes, savoring our victory and letting hope renew our strength. Hope– that we might soon be completely free and safe! And then, to Kenya, reunited with our children, and what was left of our family! It had seemed cruel to even dream about such things before now.

We would make one final crawl, towards freedom.

Chapter 9
Daybreak

"I want to work to save every child out there. And I know the president does, and I know the American people do. But neither we nor the international community have the resources nor the mandate to do so. So we have to make distinctions. We have to ask the hard questions about where and when we can intervene. And the reality is that we cannot often solve other people's problems..."

-Anthony Lake, U.S. National Security Advisor
May 5, 1994

The weather was dry and calm. The sky was starless, but there was enough moonlight that at close range I could make out the wounds and mosquito bites on poor Jeanne. The air was still thick with the foul odor of the dead, and rung with the faraway cries of wild dogs, howling like tortured souls. Jeanne smiled, for the first time in what seemed like years.

"Now that we've reached these fields," she grinned, "there is hope that we can get to the Stadium."

"If we don't delay. The Institute, remember, is occupied by the FAR. We'll be traveling directly by it. There may be soldiers in the fields, and we won't be able to see them. We have to be as quiet as we can, staying under the cover of the sorghum. Try to crawl right behind me, and I will try to clear the path for you. I am going to turn to avoid the IAMSEA as much as possible, so keep up. We only have to get to the stadium before daylight."

In spite of her courage, I could see that she was in visible pain, and worn down by sheer exhaustion.

"We only need one more miracle, my love."

We held hands and prayed silently, committing our souls to Christ, come what may. From the moment we'd first set out from Gaetan's door until now, hushed prayer had been as constant as breathing, and our every new breath depended on it. We prayed for wisdom, for courage, and for serenity, and I had often found myself silently humming an old song or hymn at moments during our flight when alertness or action made conscious prayer impossible.

Our spirits thus enriched, we started our slow slog towards the stadium, between the fence of the IAMSEA and the curve of the open road.

We hadn't advanced five meters when an explosion boomed above and behind, halting us.

A fireball streaked across the sky directly overhead. Our field was illuminated, as bright as noon. I could clearly make out a small insect, moving along the ground in front of me.

186

We froze. I was no military man, but knew that the explosion above us was a flare, used to locate hidden enemies in the nighttime. I had seen such a thing in an American movie, only a few months before.

Someone, at some point, had recognized us as we made our escape. They were hunting us.

As long as the flare's light persisted, any movement we made would be noticed. We might as well have been hiding in that open field in broad daylight! I chided myself over the trail that we'd surely left in the dust alongside that roadblock. The Interahamwe must have realized that someone had crept past their barricade. It would be a simple matter for a talented tracker to follow that path through the brush right to us.

The flare's light waned, and we scrambled onward again in the dark, spurred on by fright. But a second flare boomed– and another brilliant flood illuminated us. We were stopped cold once again.

This second time, however, there was some gain to be had from our misfortune! In our haste we had almost crawled directly into a waste-gutter that stretched all the way across the field. It was inches in front of us. The canal's edge was steeply angled, and it was twice as deep as my height. Without the light of that flare, we likely would have tumbled into it, our journey ended.

As lucky as we were to have seen the danger, the massive ditch presented a new obstacle. As the second flare dimmed, I stole a glance along the canal in both directions. It drained the waste water from the University Institute, and continued past the road. Trying to go around it in either direction would lead us straight into our enemies' hands. I could leap across it, but Jeanne, in her condition, wouldn't stand a chance at doing the same. And there was little time to lose– the FAR were hunting for us, probably at our heels.

I looked frantically around for something to use as a bridge for Jeanne. A plank of wood, perhaps. There was nothing. I could only possibly create a bridge by using *myself* as one. The physics of such a scheme were implausible, but at the level of desperation in which we found ourselves, we would have to succeed at it by pure will.

I write this account fifteen years after the Rwandan genocide, but even at this present moment, I can vividly remember the horrible strain, the mad desperation of that crawl through the sorghum field! The sweat; the pain of attempting the impossible or else facing death! I cannot, here in the present, contain the tears of emotion! My heart beats as wildly as it did then.

Here, then, is what happened: with hardly a word of explanation to Jeanne (there was no time, nor anything left to discuss), I stood and fell over the channel, landing with my hands on the opposite side. I was tall enough that my feet and ankles could rest on one bank, and my shoulders on the other, where I braced myself with my hands. The pressure on my shins and on my feet was unbearable. I would have to remain stiff enough for Jeanne to use me as a human bridge.

If we'd had more time to consider our plans, we would probably have hesitated and fallen. As it happened, Jeanne stepped across me fairly quickly, considering her dizzying pain and weakness, and tumbled to the ground by my head. I trembled and nearly blacked out at the strain of keeping my legs and body straight underneath her. Once I felt that she had crossed, my legs caved in and I nearly collapsed into the canal, only surviving by bracing my feet against its edge and kicking myself forwards. My elbows dug into the ground; I launched my right knee upwards and over the bank with them. Jeanne helped me to clamber upwards. We dragged one another into the shelter of the sorghum, and collapsed there, heaving.

Lying on our backs, side by side, we both tried to recover our minds and breath. There were hundreds of meters to go before we would see the longed-for fence surrounding the Amahoro National Stadium. Just a short distance to one side was Macadam Road– how quick and easy our trip to the stadium would be if we could only walk there, in the open!

And how difficult it was to continue to crawl, like hunted animals, inch by inch, at every moment vulnerable to venomous snakes, and searched for by armed killers!

If we were truly being hunted, then our pursuers were on the wrong trail, because it was an uneventful and dull four hours and five-hundred meters that awaited us after that fleeting rest. We pulled ourselves by our hands and elbows, through soil, plants, torturous mosquitoes, and more of the same. Our limbs felt as weak as water, our only strength coming from the knowledge that each lurch forward brought us closer to freedom and rest. The surrounding area was quiet enough; we heard no enemies shouting or trampling through the fields. The only sounds were insects, barking dogs, and our own drudgery against nature. Labored breathing... grasping against sorghum plants...spitting away dust.

Jeanne's struggles became more pronounced. Her cuts and bruises were rubbed raw. She began to moan.

"I can't take it any longer. My knees and elbows...please at least let me go to the edge of the road and walk. I'll be careful..."

It was all I could do to resist granting her request, even knowing that it would endanger her life all the more. "It would be too dangerous. Someone will see you there."

She stopped moving forward and lay still. I came closer.

"We will rest a moment," I reassured her. "When we go on, try crawling on your back or side a bit. It will be slower, but we must keep moving forwards. All of your pain is about to pay off."

In this slower fashion, we reached a clearing where there was a second road– a driveway leading to the Remera educational buildings. We were encouraged by another stroke of good luck– on this street, there was no Interahamwe roadblock, and no soul in view.

With no one watching us, we forewent acting casual and simply walked across quickly on all fours, diving into the field at the other side. I was beginning to worry about our slower pace. We were taking longer and longer to cover shorter distances, and if we risked another rest we might not reach the stadium before daylight.

Now parallel to us was a brick-making facility, owned by a Chinese company. Without taking the risk of rising out of the field to look towards the stadium, I guessed that we were only two-hundred meters away from our final goal. I whispered as such out loud, to encourage Jeanne.

It was about four 'o clock in the early morning.

We had passed the Office of Education buildings and left the IAMSEA behind us. Ahead of us loomed the National Stadium. I turned to suggest that we take a short break followed by one final crawl towards freedom, but my words were interrupted by a spray of deafening gunfire.

The shooting was coming from the Office of Education, and they were shooting directly at us.

The automatic fire pinned us to the ground. The bullets whizzed over us and around us. We pressed ourselves down against the earth, eyes closed, anticipating the sting of a bullet striking, bringing death. I wished that the ground could open up and swallow us; there was no other safe direction in which to hide. A blanket of shells in flight covered us with fire and noise, narrowly passing over our heads.

I don't recall how long the shooting lasted, but it did stop. I blinked and squinted, and so, it seemed, I had survived, though my senses were useless. My ears were ringing and all of sight, space, and direction was a blur, through which I swam in a cloud of grey smoke. Time seemed to be moving at half-speed. I could hear nothing. In this surreal state, I wondered if I had actually been killed, and passed out of my mortal body.

Several minutes later my senses had mostly recovered. I was able to move my head and make out blades of dry grass through the haze. Jeanne was no longer next to me. She had rolled away from me after the shooting started. But she couldn't be far. I whispered for her.

"Jeanne."

No answer.

"Jeanne," I whispered more boldly. "Are you alright?"

Again no reply.

I forgot about caution and danger. I lifted my head above the sorghum and looked in the direction the spray of bullets had come from. Other than the fog of grey gun-smoke still drifting through the night air, I could see nothing. I began to shout for my wife.

"Jeanne! Where are you? Say something!"

Three times more I shouted for her, but she did not– could not– answer.

I collapsed back into the brush on my back. She was gone.

Gone!

And so close to salvation at the National Stadium!

All fear and reason had left me, swept away by rage and despair, and hatred. I hated myself, and all the world. I hated the prospect of continuing on and perhaps succeeding, surviving, alone. I fell down again on my back, too defeated to move and too afraid to search for what remained of Jeanne.

I don't want it anymore. I will wait here, instead, until the Rwandan Armed Forces find me. I will let sleep take me at last. Perhaps I will never have to awaken...

How many times had Jeanne and I escaped capture or death, together? How much had we endured, together, only for her to die like this? It was too unfair to contemplate. Unfair! Better to slip into unconsciousness now, and escape this greatest cruelty of all...

I let my eyes close. A voice like Jeanne's called my name. If I died now, I could go to where she was...

It was calling me again, more clearly.

My eyes opened, I could see the waning moon and the tips of plants. The voice was an earthly one. As carelessly as before, I tried calling out loudly to Jeanne again.

"Jeanne, are you there? Can you hear me?"

"Quiet, you will get us shot."

I heard her stirring in the sorghum. A few seconds later, and she was visible an arm's length away, as alive as before.

"You were not hit, Charles?"

"No. I thought you were gone. You're okay?"

"I am safe," she moaned. "But I feel half dead, Charles." She slumped back onto the ground. "I cannot finish."

"No, darling. As long as you stay alive, all will be well..." I wanted her closer to me, but she seemed unwilling to move another inch. She was breathing in gasps. She sobbed.

"I can't take any more, Charles. Let me die here."

I dragged myself to her side.

"You cannot die. It is a miracle that you're still here with me. Surely you will make it if you try."

She shook her head. "We have wandered into a camp of the FAR, Charles. They know we are here. We are going to die."

"No, no. Look, they've stopped shooting. I don't know why, but they've stopped! Maybe they can't see us from there. We can go back closer to the road, and maybe get past them..."

"No."

She had fallen into the same gloom that had taken me only moments before. I was nearly in tears with relief at her survival, and renewed by the need to motivate her somehow. But I had little to offer.

"I will not move from here." She wept freely now. "I am bleeding everywhere. Better to just die than to go on in pain and be killed anyway..."

I hadn't seen her this despondent before. I will never forget that terrible moment, so pivotal for both of us, as I grasped and prayed for something to do, something to say, that could push her onwards. I could not carry or drag her. The soldiers were surely already moving towards us, or waiting to open fire again at our first movement. We could either crawl or die.

"Jeanne, remember the voice that I said I heard, when we were hiding in the outhouse? I didn't want to make a fuss over it, but it was real. I heard it as clear as I can hear you. It said that we would have a lot of trouble, but would not die. I know that it was a voice from God, Jeanne. I know! I don't know why we are supposed to live, but we are going to live! We are not dead yet, and we are almost safe! If you crawl with me to the stadium, we will live to tell our story to others. To our children!"

I paused to gauge her reaction, but could not make out her features in the dark. Her body did not move. I continued. "I am going on to the stadium. If you don't come with me, then I am very sorry. I have no choice...but to go alone."

With that, I swiveled around and resumed my crawl forward. Before I had traveled two meters, I heard Jeanne moaning behind me, trying to keep up. I slowed down, saying not a word– but rejoicing privately that the gambit had worked. We were on the move again.

What confused me to no end was the behavior of the soldiers. They had fired directly on us, yet we were unharmed. And now, they were silent, and didn't seem to be in pursuit. Surely they were in force here outside the stadium, and our chances of getting inside safely were slim. At any moment we expected them to burst in upon us, or to begin firing again. And yet, as long as they didn't, we continued inching closer to our goal.

Jeanne seemed to understand the finality of our situation, though her body and spirit were broken. She kept pace admirably. We made our progress more recklessly than before, eager to put distance between ourselves and the mysteriously-behaving gunmen. Our progress was rewarded by the sight of the small football field adjacent to the Amahoro National Stadium. It meant that we were almost there.

There was a clearing in our field, wherein we could see the pits dug by the Chinese construction company, for gathering soil used to make bricks. Wanting to see the best route to the stadium, I emerged from amid the sorghum near these pits, looking towards the stadium fence.

Just an arm's length away from me, I was startled by several men, armed and in military uniforms, leaping out of one of those pits, and taking cover in the nearby bushes. It looked as if I had surprised them. I retreated, stumbling back into the cover of the field.

Jeanne had seen and heard them as well. The enemy was now both ahead of us and behind us, and we could do nothing. Our position was no secret anymore.

We held each other, waiting for what would surely be our violent end– two nameless Tutsi survivors, journeying all the way to the stadium only to be killed at the very door. But ten minutes passed, and then twenty. Mosquitos buzzed about our heads and bodies, biting us freely. We didn't dare to move. Inwardly we said what we suspected were our final prayers.

I listened intently in the direction the soldiers had fled. I expected to hear them advance from there, or fire. Instead there was nothing.

I craned my neck slightly, risking a look towards the stadium. If God were truly on our side, we could make a mad dash for it if they attacked...we were pinned, after all, only a hundred meters away from rescue! It was maddening to imagine being gunned down, a short sprint's distance from safety.

A rooster crowed. They sky overhead had changed from black to dark blue.

And from the opposite direction, came footsteps.

Two uniformed men were coming into the field from the road, rifles hanging at their sides. Now they were stomping through the sorghum in heavy boots. I could hear bits of their conversation.

"I had them dead in my targets."

"They must not have passed here."

They were walking directly towards us. We flattened ourselves against the ground, trembling. I could hear one of them bring his gun into firing position.

They broke into the clearing made by our prone bodies. One of them stepped directly by my side, and narrowly missed tripping over me. But he did not look down. The two of them continued on, away from us.

For another ten minutes we could hear them tramping about in the field, growing gradually farther away.

Our hiding place was about to become useless– dawn was breaking. From about thirty meters behind us came soldiers' voices once again. They might have been the same men who were shooting at us. I could hear them talking.

"Do you see? They went this way."

"I'm sure we shot them. See the blood here? They must have crawled off to die."

"Or they are wounded. Be careful."

They had found our trail through the field. It would lead directly to us.

It occurred to me only at that moment that the voices had spoken in the Swahili language. In my panic I hadn't recognized the significance of this at first. The government army only spoke Kinyarwanda, or French. These soldiers, then, might be FPR rebels!

They were quickly following our trail now. In a few seconds, they would be upon us.

I waited until they were only ten meters away, and I could see them. Their guns were at the ready. They would spot us any moment now. I could view their uniforms. They were Inkotanyi for certain– but they mistook us for FAR troops or scouts, or Interahamwe thugs. Once they saw us, they would probably open fire. Our entire night's journey could end with both of us dead at the hands of allies!

My mind raced wildly in every direction. Should I stand up and call out for mercy? Should I hold still and remain quiet, so they don't shoot in surprise? There was no time to choose! Instead of deciding on a course of action, my mind went blank. I was completely paralyzed.

"We are Tutsi! Don't shoot please!"

The startled soldiers pivoted and pointed their rifles, but did not fire. The sound of a woman's voice had given them pause. It was Jeanne, sitting up and quite bravely entreating them.

I joined her in pleading our case.

"Stand up. Hands on your heads," said one of them.

We tried to obey quickly, but only stumbled to our knees instead. The fatigue and starvation had caught up to us.

One of the rebels lowered his gun, and offered a hand instead.

"Are you okay? Neither of you are wounded?"

"No," I stammered back, as Jeanne said the same. "We weren't hit by any bullets."

"Well!" He took a step backwards, as if to have a better look at us. "Damn my foot! That's not possible! Are you sure neither of you has been shot?"

They circled us, inspecting us from head to toe excitedly.

"Well, I can see it now," he shrugged, "but I don't believe it. And you came here from Kimironko? Are you husband and wife?"

They blitzed us with questions, all the while gawking at us as if we were ghosts in human disguise. We must have looked as much. I was eager only to be helped into the stadium and to safety, but the two young men were as relaxed as if they were on holiday. They made us explain our story to them again and again, and then called loudly to some of their companions, only to ask us to repeat the tale for them as well. I politely protested.

"I'm sorry, but we are starving and haven't had any sleep. My wife needs medical attention. We've been crawling all the way through the field."

This had the desired effect. They gave us their shoulders to cling to, and walked us towards the stadium, still milling about us curiously as they went.

I was lightheaded and could hardly keep pace, feeling as though I was drifting in and out of consciousness. My head spinning, I was aware of Jeanne beside me. She was practically being dragged along.

Another one of the rebels came alongside and addressed me as we went. "Your name is Charles?"

"Yes."

"Mr. Charles, why did you crawl through the field instead of walking on the road?"

"We did not want to be seen by the Interahamwe, or the army."

Several of them broke into a laugh; a few others appeared quite sorry for us.

In a combination of Swahili and Kinyarwandan, they said to us the sweetest words to reach our ears in a long, long time:

"Poleni saana djameni, hivi baasi mukae bila wasi yoyote, tena mupumuzike katika mwoyoni kwenu, juu tangu hivi tatizo zenu zinaishilia hapa. Nitwe runyenzi mwajyaga mwumva, askali ya RPF. Kwa hive munakalibiwa saana."

Meaning, in English: "We are very sorry for that, but from now on you can relax, for your worries are over. We are the so-called cockroaches, the FPR. Welcome home."

Chapter 10
Commando

"Acts of genocide may have been committed."

-United Nations Security Council, during discussions over whether to intervene in Rwanda. Opposing an intervention, the American Secretary of State then delayed the vote for four days.

May 13, 1994

As we sagged off of the arms of our new benefactors, half-walking, half-dragged towards the stadium, they told us that the area was completely under their control. It was the FPR who had fired upon us, mistaking us for scouts of the Rwandan Armed Forces.

"The FAR killed every Tutsi in Kimironko long ago. We were expecting their army to try to cross the field, to take back the stadium. That is why we defended it so heavily. We never would have guessed that a couple of Tutsi survivors would still be there, and would try to sneak through our minefield."

"Minefield?" I nearly lost consciousness.

Jeanne had heard it, too.

A moment later, soldiers were rushing to bring us some more water, quite certain that we were both going mad. We had burst into laughter.

Minutes later we were seated inside the National Stadium, stiff and shaking. Some of the men ran to bring some biscuits for us, and to bring back bandages and antiseptic for Jeanne's wounds.

The remaining soldiers quizzed me again about our escape from Kimironko. It was May the 3rd; nearly a month after the massacres had begun on April 7th. How had we survived among the killers for so long, and how did we know to come to the stadium once it had been taken by the rebels? How did we get away from the Interahamwe?

I told them our story from the beginning, about the assault upon our home on the morning of April 7th, about our flight to the home of Dr. Alphonse Biramvu, and then to that of the ordinary Hutu man who became our angel, Gaetan. I told them about the eighteen days spent hiding in a hole of eight meters, about our hiding in the outhouses of cottages, and finally, the last flight across the barricades into the FPR minefield.

"You are incredibly lucky!" the oldest gentleman among them, in his mid-thirties, whistled and spat on the ground. He was especially impressed to hear that we had crawled through the minefield and survived his colleagues' own machine-gun fire.

"In all my life I have never seen anything like this. It looks like magic!"

Another added, "Well, you certainly were born with a star on the front. You're in good hands now, rest assured. And don't worry about those tormentors of yours. We'll get them."

They kept pressing me for more details about our adventures. They seemed especially curious about Jeanne. At each part of the story they interrupted to ask, What about your wife? Was she afraid? What did she do? How did she manage it? She would be quite proud of herself had she been able to hear it, but she'd been laid on her side, fast asleep.

I was grateful when the questioning ended, as Jeanne was awakened and we were once again each propped up between two soldiers, still unable to walk under our own power. They brought us to a detachment post to provide us with several biscuits, blankets and clean clothes. We felt as if we had risen out of the grave, into sunlight, back again from the dead.

It was after five o'clock in the morning. The third day of May, 1994, a date and time that I will never forget. It had been nine hours since we left Gaetan's house, intending to flee Kimironko or die in the attempt. Entirely by the grace of God, we had succeeded.

I will be certain to tell everyone that You have brought us here, I thought. *I must not forget. We will never forget. We are truly thankful, Lord.*

We were told that the National Stadium had become a transitory camp for fugitives looking for safety from the fighting, both Hutu and Tutsi alike. UNAMIR, the U.N.'s operation in Rwanda, was present, hosted by the FPR who also kept forces at the stadium for protection. The stadium, I was told, was one of a tiny handful of U.N. safe-havens left in Rwanda. A force of only a few hundred poorly-equipped peacekeepers remained in the country. The rest had been removed at the beginning of the genocide.

And a true genocide it was. No one was certain about the number of the dead, but it seemed as though there were few Tutsis left in the world. Some said that half a million had perished, others a million.

(All killed while the United States and her allies continued to deny that there was "officially" a genocide at all! One particular trick of the U.S. State Department at the time was to only refer to "acts of genocide" taking place in Rwanda, carefully circumventing an actual admission of "genocide" that would have required aid and action. They not only declined to prevent the slaughter– they campaigned, forcefully, for a complete withdrawal of peacekeepers, insisting that the world let the massacres play out just as the Interahamwe hoped; watching and hearing of the carnage only from a safe distance. The two or three hundred UNAMIR men remaining– in the entire country– could do little more than assist what few survivors were sheltered behind the FPR battle-lines.)

Our own survival-story was quickly spreading through the camp. As we gratefully let ourselves be carried away to where we could rest, officers and soldiers alike came to catch a glimpse of us– the two civilians who had survived among the Hutu militia, run through bullets, and crawled by luck through the FPR's own minefield.

Jeanne in particular found herself becoming the center of interest. They admired her as if she were an angel; they whispered to one another about her exploits.

There is the woman who crawled, bleeding, for fifteen hundred meters to arrive safely here!

The woman who outsmarted the Interahamwe for four weeks!

Her story was taking on mythic proportions. They gave her the impromptu nickname "Commando" and in a matter of hours, she was known as such by everyone on the grounds.

We were impatient to sleep, to shower, and to put on our fresh new clothes. But they informed us that we were not to stay at the stadium for long. We were to be moved in about half an hour, they said, to a safer place. *A safer place? Safer than this?* I felt more safe than I'd ever been in my life, right where I was! The stadium, in fact, might as well have been heaven. We saw no need to be transported; we would have preferred to fall down and sleep immediately. But there was no use protesting. The officer attending to us explained that the FAR kept a steady barrage of mortar fire upon the stadium. They had taken many lives, and were expected to make an attempt at reclaiming the place. As he went on describing the situation, I began to grasp his point. Though I felt a relative peace and joy inside these walls, it surely was not safe.

The officers led us to an area where there was a practice field for football (or as the Americans know it, soccer.) In the center of the field a fire was burning, and the smell of the smoke scarcely masked the awful but familiar odor of dead bodies. There were dozens of them, laid side by side in organized heaps, as far as possible from the living. Refugees mostly, I was told, who had found safety in the stadium only to be killed by the mortar fire of the FAR. We did not ask our guides about the identity of those unfortunate ones, nor did we wish to know.

"You two wait here. Some vehicles will be ready soon to take you away." They left us alone on a veranda, surrounded by tents where badly wounded refugees were cared for by a few haggard-looking aid workers. The mortar attacks kept everyone huddled as close to the center of the stadium as possible. They gasped and shouted collectively every time the distinctive discharge of a mortar was heard. The FPR, meanwhile, patrolled and circled the stadium in shifts, keeping the enemy at a far enough distance to encumber their aim. The rebels had the advantage of numbers and position, and could come and go from the stadium in force, though at great risk.

We had a quiet moment to ourselves, waiting for the start of the perilous journey to whatever place our protectors deemed "safer". Jeanne was resting in the shade on her side, and I occupied myself watching the rebel soldiers, UNAMIR troops, and refugees coming and going. The FPR men, more than the others, were especially enraged by the mortar fire; they fumed and cursed the FAR, and the Hutu in general, vowing to punish them in the cruelest ways possible, and with every kind of violent oath.

It was a distressing atmosphere for those few Hutu refugees in the stadium. I could see them nervously keeping in groups to themselves, preferring to be near the U.N. peacekeepers and aid workers from abroad. If one of the Inkotanyi addressed them with any orders or questions, they jumped to their feet and obeyed quickly, eager to please. Still the FPR soldiers only spoke shortly and inhospitably to them, often with an insult and an air of open disgust. I wondered how many of those maltreated Hutu were like noble Gaetan, deplorers of tribalism and violence. The illogical hatred between so-called "Hutu" and "Tutsi" was in full effect here in this place of refuge, and the deaths of hundreds of thousands in our streets seemed to have imparted no lesson at all.

Growing restless, I walked casually in circles among the refugees, stretching my aching limbs, always keeping the veranda in view along with my sleeping wife. I was curious to hear from the soldiers and officers about the operations in the stadium, and to learn about the war still raging outside. I heard confusing snatches of conversation between the rebel soldiers; they spoke of clearings and isolations and spies. I began to realize that they were concerned about Interahamwe or their collaborators hiding among them, posing as innocent

Hutu refugees. It was the topic of most of their private discussions.

The time came for our transport. We were brought before a high-ranking officer, escorted by two bodyguards. He introduced himself as Afande Nkusi. He was the officer responsible for the military operations in that unit of Remera. We greeted him with the customary respect.

He asked us a series of questions about our identity and situation. Once we had answered to his satisfaction, we were told to rise and follow. As he turned away I heard him make a radio-call, instructing a driver to come and move us with all possible care. My eyes widened at his final order:

"These two are Tutsi. Take them to the CND, to Major Kayonga."

To where–and to whom? To our old friend Afande Charles?

Apart from the joy of perhaps seeing a familiar face again, the Afande's words raised even more questions that we didn't dare to ask out loud. Had the rebels successfully defended the CND the entire time? How much of Kigali had they taken? Were they going to win the war?

The National Development Council building was, of course, well-known to us. If it was still the FPR headquarters, and if we could so freely drive there, it could only mean good things for the prospect of an end to this genocide. The CND was well-situated, and we would truly be able to rest in safety there. And if the roads between here and there were also secure, then perhaps the war would soon be over, and the FPR victorious...

Naive as I was, I imagined the rebel forces negotiating peace and helping to restore order to Rwanda...perhaps the shame and horror of the genocide would bring a new reconciliation and harmony between Hutu and Tutsi. I thought about the Germans– only fifty years ago responsible for the notorious genocide known as the holocaust, now at peace and determined never to repeat the disgraces of the past.

Surely the tension here at the stadium between Hutu and Tutsi is only because the fighting is still going on...emotions are just running high. Once the world sees what has happened here, Rwanda can change. There won't be Hutu and Tutsi anymore, not after this. Only fellow Rwandans...

Fifty years from now, Rwanda itself could be just as prosperous, just as committed to equality as Germany, couldn't it? There could be beauty for ashes...

My head stayed filled with lofty hopes until we were guided into a pickup truck and driven away. It was still early morning, and the Amahoro stadium was behind us now, as was the football field strewn with corpses, the sorghum laced with explosives...

The truck reached the familiar Chez-Lando intersection, turning right. It was only a five-minute drive from there to the CND...a drive I remembered taking only four weeks ago, in a more peaceful age.

The familiar drive had now become a tour of horrors. Bodies were left in heaps all around, in various states of decay. To see such a thing in the daylight was an awful new experience, one that brought our heads down and made us shudder. We closed our eyes, holding back tears.

The CND and its entrances were heavily guarded, and surrounded by soldiers at the ready. We gratefully accepted their help climbing from the parked vehicle, and were guided past a gauntlet of armed Inkotanyi, ducking into the side entrance as if we were taking shelter from the war outside. Here we would find rest, and comfort.

My idealistic dreams for the future gave way for a moment to thoughts of the National Stadium, and the Hutus taking shelter there from the violence. I couldn't help but wonder whether Gaetan was safe, wherever he was.

Chapter 11
The Exodus

"Has the administration yet come to any decision on whether it can be described as genocide?"

"I'll have to confess, I don't know the answer to that. I know that the issue was under very active consideration."

-Mike McCurry, U.S. State Department press briefing
May 25, 1994

We were escorted by a young soldier into what was to be our new home. It was a spacious unfurnished room, with a stack of mattresses against one wall. There were bags and boxes spilling over with clothes, old shoes and various household items. The area was used to store donations made by FPR sympathizers, for their first arrival into Kigali.

Our young guide set down his rifle and pulled two mattresses out from near the top of the heap. Rummaging through the bundles of items along the opposite wall, he emerged with two wool blankets of good quality.

"Follow me now," he addressed me as he re-shouldered his gun, "I'll show you where the lavatories are, where you can take a shower."

A shower! We were still caked with the mud and dirt of three weeks. He might as well have offered us a fortune in gold. With a new spring in my step I limped behind him through a series of identical-looking corridors, arriving at a door marked "TOILET' in gigantic letters.

"You can shower first," he said, "and then invite your wife. In fact, if you like I can bring her now."

I told him that I would be delighted if he could bring her, thanking him profusely. He turned and left me there, alone in that cold and wonderful bathroom.

There was a mirror above the sink. I drew near to it with some trepidation, curious to see what had become of my face. And though I was expecting to see something unpleasant, my own reflection was still quite a shock. I was unrecognizable, even to myself!

Facing me in that mirror was not a man but a disfigured sort of zombie. I was rail-thin, my bones all visible when I removed my shirt. Worse, my skin was torn and yellowish, covered with brown and red spots. My gaunt face, especially, was swollen with mosquito bites accrued from our night crawling through the minefield. To think that such a deformed skeleton could be a walking, living man!

I sighed at my condition. And then, beside me in the mirror, was the ghost of Jeanne, pouting at her own reflection as I stared into my own, riveted. She hardly resembled the beautiful woman I had always known! Here was a soul bent over by the crushing weight of suffering, hunger, and thirst, only weakly clinging to life.

Her head and body were also blistered with cuts, scrapes and bruises, mingled with the redness and swelling from mosquito bites. They had deformed her face; it was weary from a long and winding journey through hell. The joy had been erased from her countenance. Furrows of mud had collected in her hair and dried, from the days spent hiding in the pit, and her eyes sagged from the accumulated nights with neither sleep nor peace. Only the faintest spark, the weak but enduring light of the soul of the woman I knew, remained, inextinguishable. She was broken, but still resolutely herself.

Our young soldier was standing at the bathroom doorway, curiously watching our reaction to the sight of ourselves. I turned to thank him, and to request that he return in an hour to show us the way back to our rooms. I had already quite forgotten the path through the winding hallways.

He obliged, and left us alone. Like children at Christmas, we pounced on the sweet-smelling bars of soap and fresh water.

Please try to imagine the heavenly experience that was our first real shower in weeks! The steaming jets of warm water not only cleaned our bodies, but seemed to restore us to civilization; to a world we had lost. We had, over the last month, transformed into hunted feral animals, estranged from the world of human pleasantness– of books and music, plates and knives, of friendship and leisure. Of all the lost comforts of our old lives, only God Himself remained with us in the brush, when all other joys and pleasures had departed. Now, as we scrubbed away the caked-on dirt and watched it pool into muddy water at our feet, we could feel our old selves reemerge from underneath. Our torments, those things which he had seen and could never forget, no longer clung to us so tightly. The memory of them fled down the drain along with the dirt of the fields. Our scars might never fade, but they could, to some extent, be scrubbed clean.

I understand how a shower can be taken for granted, when enjoyed nearly every day of one's life. It's both natural and forgivable, if you cannot fathom the unspeakable joy of that first shower of ours, at the headquarters of the National Development Council. But it was a moment for which I'll forever be thankful!

As no towels were available at the time, we were wrapped in wax Dutch paper by the time our guide returned to take us back to our room to change. It was as if we were being escorted by the angels, to our new quarters in heaven.

And there, on the floor, were two plates and two bowls of hot soup! We had reveled in our shower so happily that we'd forgotten how terribly hungry we were. The young soldier served us rice and meat, politely and quietly, deftly plating our food while lighting a new cigarette for himself. Our stomachs growled.

He was about to crack open a can of beer for us when we interjected.

"It's alright," I said. "We will have something else."

"We've got all kinds of wine. If you want some, please don't hesitate to let me know."

"Thank you," I replied. "We will be really happy with just water."

He nodded and slipped out the door. We were about to dive into our feast when he returned, to our surprise, holding a variety of sodas: Coke and orange and lemon Fanta. A *Kadogo*– a boy soldier, no older than fifteen– was with him, with his own rifle hanging from his shoulder, and a plastic bag in his hand. From it he brought forth a package of biscuits, and a metal container of powdered milk, which he explained could be mixed with the porridge we'd be served each morning.

Who are we to deserve this kind of treatment here?
We wondered without words, overwhelmed.

They wished us good appetite, and promised to visit us again as soon as possible.

Jeanne and I were left alone, looking over our feast. For the first time since the 6th of April, a genuine grin formed on both our faces.

Late that afternoon, we were lost together in a deep, contented sleep. Someone came knocking discreetly at the door. It was a new pair of soldiers, offering us an assortment of personal and cosmetic items, as well as two bottles of wine.

Over their protests, we explained to them that we did not drink alcohol.

"Very well," one of them relented. "We will inform the Afande that you don't drink. He is the one who wanted us to make sure that we offered you anything you'd like."

With that, they were gone. I was curious to know who exactly this Afande was who had taken such an interest in us. Could it be my friend Charles Kayonga, the original commander of the entire battalion stationed here? How could he have had time to learn about our story, while combat still raged in the city? I was not yet bold enough to ask the soldiers attending to us who our generous benefactor was, or to ask to meet with him. I wanted to learn whether we might be able to leave Rwanda at some point, to go to our children. I wanted to talk to someone who could ensure Gaetan's safety back in Kimironko. I wanted to learn which, if any, of our family and friends had survived. But now was not the time to ask any more favors.

We soon had plenty of guests to drink the beer and wine that we'd politely refused. The two young Inkotanyi never left our room, and were quickly joined by other soldiers, and then by still more. They were all curious to see us, and to ask us questions about our adventures.

By late in the evening we had told the story several times, always receiving compliments and words of comfort in return. It was a pleasant atmosphere there in our new quarters, surrounded by friendly company, smiling and having noisy conversation without the fear of capture and death hovering over us! More than once I found myself thinking about those silent, suspenseful mealtimes we had shared with Gaetan's family, and hoping that I someday might have a jovial time of fellowship with them as well, in an age of peace.

It was a surreal thing to pass so quickly out of a world of hatred– of racism, murder, the torture and death of children– and into a place filled with this kind of friendship and comfort. It gave pause to my joy, even as our kindly guests, one by one, began to politely excuse themselves for the night.

Stacking our two mattresses on top of one another, Jeanne and I slept through the night, in perfect peace.

The next morning we were informed that we would be meeting with the officer who had given orders for our care. We searched through the piles of clothes in the room, looking for suitable outfits for the occasion. Like children, we laughed and joked as we modeled clothing for one another, admiring our new fashions. It was still fairly early in the day when we were taken to meet the Afande.

It was not Charles Kayonga whom we met that morning. This gentleman– Afande David– was, we learned, newly in command of the supply chain for the CND, and for all the FPR units fighting in the capital city. We were impressed by his caring manner, as he bid us sit down and tell him, from the beginning, the story of our journey surviving the genocide.

I launched into our tale, taking special care to mention Gaetan by name, and to emphasize his heroism and kindness towards us. He listened attentively as we told about our many miraculous brushes with death, and our will to survive, fueled by faith and the longing to be reunited with our children. I ended by thanking him heartily for all that he'd done for us in the past two days.

"Think nothing of it," he replied, although he was clearly pleased by our gratitude. "You can be sure now that your troubles are over. As for your kids, leaving the country is just not possible now. This is still a time of war. But whenever things are more peaceful around here, you can go to them, or they can come home to you. In the meantime, let me know if you need anything, and I promise that I will come and visit you whenever I have the opportunity."

As we were ushered back towards our quarters, we both agreed that this Afande David was a remarkably good fellow.

I had begun to regain my balance, and was able to walk at my normal pace again. I spent the rest of the morning walking among the hallways, rooms, and bathrooms of the CND, looking for anyone I knew among the other survivors scattered about. One elderly man, I thought, looked very much like my old history teacher, but as I approached him, he did not seem to recognize me. I decided that it was only a close resemblance.

I rejoined Jeanne in our room that afternoon, where, at about four o' clock, we were ordered to take shelter in the basement along with all of the other civilians. The fighting between the FPR and the Rwandan army had reached our block.

Soldiers herded us down the stairs into the crowded basement. As soon as we had joined the other huddled refugees below the ground, a sound like thunder exploded somewhere above us. The floor and walls trembled. The FAR were launching mortars at the building.

"It's nothing to worry about. We're safe here. The FAR have bombed this area before. But they're getting weaker."

Smiling by my side was the old man I had passed by in the hallway earlier. He was, indeed, my old history professor. There was no mistaking him now that we stood face to face.

213

"Charles– forgive me," he said, "I wasn't sure that it was you whom I saw this morning. You have lost so much weight, and look so very different. Have you been alright?"

We waited out the bombing by sharing our respective stories. His was a simple one– he was already at the CND, participating in a military training exercise, when the missile attack destroyed the president's plane. He had stayed safe inside ever since.

I was happy to meet at least one soul whom I recognized. When the danger of the bombing was past, he accompanied us back to our room, and we talked throughout the evening. I quizzed him for information on whether any of our friends or relatives had passed through, but he recognized none of their names.

Each morning we slept in late, awakened by a soldier assigned to take care of us. Each day we took a morning shower, a hearty breakfast, and chatted with the soldiers and new friends we had made among the civilians. Conversations always turned towards rumors of the war, the progress being made by the FPR, and the retreat of the government forces from strategic positions. Word reached us that the United Nations had chosen not to come to the aid of the Tutsi. For all their fifty years of grandstanding over "never again" allowing a genocide, they had agreed to let this one run its course right under their noses, as they counted the dead in a land ostensibly under their protection.

All of our remaining hopes were with the FPR. The massacres, we heard, were still happening, and it was whispered that up to a million innocents had died. The genocide had been planned and prepared for by the Rwandan government for months. The president's death had only provided the opportunity.

We also caught word of Inkotanyi victories. The soldiers spoke of "clearing" a geographical area after it was occupied by the FPR. By this, I soon learned, they meant the elimination of what they described as pockets of Interahamwe in a region. The regions of Byumba and part of the prefecture of Ruhengeri had been taken and "cleared" in this fashion, and I listened with some trepidation as soldiers boasted of their vengeful rampages.

"Our unit was in the East of the country," one young fighter told me, "and we fought the FAR all the way to Kibungo. Then we arrived in Mukarange, where we found a church with a lot of Tutsi bodies inside. So we cleared all of the hills of Mukarange, Kayonza, Muhazi– everywhere around there. We made sure that no Hutu was left alive."

By 'Hutu' he must mean only the FAR and the Interahamwe, I reasoned, though I dared not ask aloud to make sure. Everyone else must have already fled the area. He certainly cannot mean that all of the Hutu were killed...

I took a circuitous approach. "Did you take any prisoners from there? Any Hutu civilians?"

"No, there were no civilians. Why do you ask that?"

I thought it safer to let the matter drop.

During our second week at the CND, we were visited again by Afande David.

"I would like to send you to Byumba," he announced. "We have a refugee camp set up there for genocide survivors. It's quite nice. You will be safer there, and it is completely peaceful."

As happy as we were in our present situation, Jeanne and I were both eager to accept the invitation. The bombings had become painfully loud, and Jeanne was developing headaches and having horrible nightmares of our crawl underneath the machine-gun fire outside the stadium.

"You have three days to get ready to leave," the Afande continued, "A convoy of refugees is leaving for Byumba then, under military escort. You will head out after dark, and have to go on foot all night. I wish you a safe journey."

We prepared for our trip by selecting a few changes of clothing for each of us from among the piles of clothes near our bed. I rolled up two sleeping-mats, along with several blankets and whatever other necessities we could carry.

In a refugee camp, we might meet people desperately in need of these items, I thought.

The night of our departure came, and I was examining our bundle of items with Jeanne, when a familiar person suddenly appeared behind me, in the doorway.

"Charles? I didn't believe it when they told me that you were here."

"Mugabo?" He was an old friend from my days as a bachelor.

We embraced each other, laughing. How joyful an experience, to see an old friend at a time when nearly all other loved ones have been taken from the earth!

"Jean Mugabo, you are alive? You escaped from the massacres?"

"Yes, I survived, and my dear Jeanne did too– just like yours." Mugabo's wife was also named Jeanne, and our families had remained close. "I'll tell you all about it, once we've had a drink and sat down awhile." He shook his head.

"It is good to see you both again, Charles. Jeanne will be delighted to know that you are some of the lucky ones."

He was soon seated on the floor, back to the wall, enjoying a soda. Our friendship had been a long and sincere one, beginning years ago, at a time when we were both single and seemed to nearly always be at one another's houses. We drifted apart a bit when I went to live in Kimironko and married, but we'd always kept in touch. After April 7th, I'd assumed that he and his family had been killed, like every other Tutsi. He had assumed the same regarding us. Now his smile was a mile wide.

"Afande David told me about the incredible husband and wife who outsmarted the Interahamwe and escaped to the National Stadium, but until today he never mentioned your names. Once I realized that it was you, I told him that I was going to take you to Byumba myself, right away. I have a home there; both of you shall live with us."

We were ecstatic. "But the Afande told us that we were leaving with the other refugees in the convoy, on foot. Are you sure we have permission to travel separately?"

"No problem! He knows. We're even going to find a vehicle for you to take there. Just pack up whatever you'll need, and we will go at once. Hey there! I think your car is ready right now."

Two soldiers stood in the doorway. They nodded towards Mugabo and then towards me.

"The Afande sent us. The road to Byumba is clear, and you should leave right away. The convoy is leaving in about an hour. We are to take you to pick up your new car first, at the Ministry of Education. It's a two kilometer trip. Are you ready?"

Mugabo, it seemed, was a man of some importance! Everything was happening so quickly!

Mugabo, the two soldiers, and I exited the CND and squeezed into a camouflage-colored car waiting outside. Jeanne would be waiting with our meager luggage, ready to begin the trip to Byumba as soon as we returned. It was raining heavily. My heart beat faster than it had in many days.

The Inkotanyi had an unusual and reckless way of driving by night: no headlights on; no use of the brakes. They avoided paved roads, ignored stop signs and intersections, and took shortcuts on improvised streets, all at dangerously high speeds. They were used to driving after this fashion, so as not to attract rockets or gunfire from the FAR. But for me, it was a frightening ride.

Fifty meters away from the Ministry of Education building, the cramped car slowed and rolled to a stop. The driver turned to address me.

"Here is the Ministry. Now you are going to enter the parking lot to your right. You will see a white Peugeot 305. Open the driver's side door and you will find the keys on the

217

dashboard. You will start the car and join us here. Do not turn the headlights on. Do not put your foot on the brake pedal."

They expect me to drive like this? In the rain? I already regretted leaving the relative safety of the CND. The monotone soldier continued giving instructions.

"To your right will be the station of the National Police. They fight along with the FAR. If you make the slightest error, they will spot you and shoot you."

"Should I have someone to come with me? I don't know if I am capable of this..."

"If they shoot at you, we will not wait longer than a few seconds for you. Now go– the longer we stay here, the greater the danger."

I had no choice, neither did I want to seem cowardly, though risking so much for a car struck me as foolish. I looked to Mugabo, who said nothing. I stepped out into the rain alone.

I was covered in complete darkness, and the sounds of my movements were drowned out by the pattering rain. I took courage in this, and jogged towards where the vehicles were parked. My eyes had adjusted enough to the dark that I could make out the shapes of cars.

Everything was exactly as I had been told. The white car was there, seemingly brand new. The door was unlocked, though I winced at the interior lights that glowed as I opened it. The keys were there on the dashboard. I fumbled with them in my trembling hand, and quickly sat down and turned the key in the ignition, frightened by my own light and noise, and eager to race away to safety.

The engine would not start. I adjusted the key and tried again. Something was wrong. After a fourth attempt with no success, I was certain that there was a drained battery, or some other such problem.
I ran back to rejoin the others.

"The engine will not start. There must be some electrical problem. I tried to start it several times..."

I was cut off by sharp rebuke in turn from both soldiers.

"You are a fool. You civilians–

"That vehicle starts very well on the first try. It's you– you kept messing around with the ignition. Go back over there and bring that car here. You're on your own if it happens again."

"Now stay calm, start the car, and follow us out of here."

I sheepishly made my way back, wondering what I could possibly do differently on a second attempt. I confidently plunged the key into the ignition again, and this time the engine roared to life easily. It was working quite well.

I backed up only enough to exit the parking lot gate, awkwardly changing into second gear while rolling through pitch blackness, hardly able to make out what was in front of me. As I approached the car holding the others, Mugabo appeared out in the rain, waving to me with both arms. I had no choice but to step on the brakes, and he leapt into the seat next to me.

We were startled by a loud, repeating popping sound; a pistol firing at us from the direction of the police station!

The Inkotanyi's vehicle peeled out and sped away into the rain. Mugabo and I followed frantically, afraid of losing our companions in the downpour and darkness. Without any lights, keeping them in sight was obscenely difficult, as was staying in the center of the road.

The police offered little other resistance to our flight. After the first few shots fired, and the attendant flashes, we saw and heard nothing as we left them behind us in the blackened streets.

I was on-edge enough already from trying to keep up with the wild driving technique of the soldiers. Mugabo's instructions from the passenger seat did little to help. We tried to follow from only three meters behind, so as not to lose them, or our way. We were soon back outside of the

CND, where Jeanne was waiting with our belongings. She had found larger bags in our absence, and filled them.

We would have no chance to say our goodbye to the generous Afande David. Mugabo helped us to toss our bags into back seat of our new car, and hurried Jeanne in beside me. He himself had his own car, and driver, at the ready.

Lining up out in the street was the long procession of weary and soaked refugees, ready to travel by foot all through the night, accompanied by the FPR escort, to the Byumba camp.

We waited for the departure signal inside of our new car, in comfort and shelter. I was eager to tell my wife about the adventure I'd had risking my skin to bring this prize to her, but decided that it wasn't the best time. It would probably worry her more than amuse.

Close by my window passed a woman among the gathering refugees, holding a sobbing young girl in her arms. The suffering child was inconsolable, and the sadness of the pair filled me with pity. *Surely the troops wouldn't forbid us to take a passenger with us? There is room in the back seat...*

I rolled down the window to get a better look. I thought that we could offer to take the mother and daughter with us– but discreetly, without creating jealously among the others. To my surprise, I recognized the young lady. She was Saidath; we had been friends since childhood. I knew her husband.

When did she arrive to the CND, and why did we never see her until now?

She passed by us. I called out to her by name. When she turned back, confused, I stepped out into the rain so that she could recognize me.

"Saidath– it's Charles, sister. Come into the car with us. We are also going to Byumba."

She ran and fell on my chest, bursting into tears. Her husband was nowhere to be seen.

I helped them into the seat behind us, squeezing them in among our bags. She thanked us meekly through her pain as best she could, still comforting the weeping child.

Minutes later, the miserable caravan of survivors received the signal to go on the move. The brave Inkotanyi led the way, flanked us, and kept watch over the rain-soaked mass of humanity, like uniformed shepherds. Their vehicles, and ours, stopped, waited, and rolled forwards at a crawl, always without headlights.

Our joyless parade made frequent stops, as the soldiers leading the way scouted ahead to make certain that the roads were safe and clear. We would be satisfying targets for the Interahamwe if they could reach us: the few fish who had escaped their murderous net, together and helpless.

Jeanne and I tried to make conversation with Saidath, but she was not eager to share much about her experiences, nor the fate of her husband. From what little we gathered, it was clear that she and the child had good reason to cry. We let them fall into a mournful sleep; Saidath leaning against our luggage, the child clinging to her side.

By dawn we had passed completely into FPR-controlled territory. Peace and rest were at hand, giving fresh power to the feet of those exhausted travelers. It was the morning of June 19th, 1994, when we arrived in the town of Byumba, our Promised Land. We were herded towards the town's large Catholic church, to be organized into groups and directed to separate camps prepared for us. Schools, hospitals, abandoned homes, and rental properties in Byumba had all been transformed by the FPR into dwellings for groups of survivors.

FPR authorities awaited us first, to screen each individual and gather their information. Refugees already situated in the camp were strictly ordered not to mingle or talk to the new arrivals until they had been processed, but they gathered by the church, as closely as they dared, straining their necks to see if the new convoy contained their lost relatives and friends.

We traveled along with the pedestrians, but always remaining inside the car. We could see little of the goings-on outside through the early-morning fog. Our pace was so slow that we passed time by looking for any familiar faces in the crowds. Saidath and the child had awakened and were curiously glued to the windows as well.

The few soldiers managing the throngs at the church were overwhelmed by the logistical nightmare of processing and housing so many. One of them impatiently pounded on the door of our vehicle.

"You in the car– are you not going to come out to be inspected? You're no better than anyone else here."

I stopped the car and the four of us obediently stepped out. Saidath seemed especially frightened by this rude reception.

"Everyone here is equal." He scowled. "No more bourgeois comforts for you."

The frowning soldier then looked over the car and turned to me.

"This vehicle is immediately mobilized for service in the army."

I handed him the keys without a word. It was the FPR who had given it to me, anyway. I wanted to at least explain to him that our luggage was inside, but thought better of it.

We fell in line, as instructed, with the other refugees. They were exhausted by their long overnight march. Some of them had wounds, still fresh, from machetes across their heads and bodies. Occasionally we would spot a dejected woman holding a dead or dying child.

There were some Hutu also among the refugees– those who had been known to be political moderates, who had been guilty of sheltering Tutsis, or who simply had wanted no part in the violence. They were nervous and fearful, as if expecting to be accused, rightly or wrongly, of the crimes committed by their kin.

Someone tapped me on the shoulder. It was Jean Mugabo.

"Ah, I've found you, brother."

"Mugabo, we didn't see you in the convoy."

"I went to my house first, to tell them that you were coming, and that they should prepare a room for you there. Like I told you before, you're not going to be camping in the crowd. After registration, take your car and join me at the School of Sociology."

"I will meet you there, but I no longer have a car. They took it for the army."

This news seemed to anger my friend. "Took it? Who took it from you? Can you show me who he is?"

I pointed out the man who had ordered us out of our vehicle and into the line.

Mugabo marched straight over to the man, who seemed to be an important fellow, and inflexible. They talked at length, cordially and with frequent smiles and pats of the shoulder between them, until at last the officer gave the car keys to Mugabo. The two then shook hands and bid each other farewell, having come to some sort of friendly agreement.

He returned and handed the keys to me.

"Don't bother with registration," he said. "I will ride with you and we can leave this place at once."

I remembered my poor traveling companion Saidath and her child. Scanning the line of people, I found them and ran over to them quickly, to tell her that I would be leaving right away. I promised to find her again, as soon as I could, if I could bring her something useful.

I had no time to even finish listening to her thank us for giving them a ride. We were rumbling out onto the road, with Mugabo directing me from the passenger side, and Jeanne seated behind. Mugabo continued to fascinate us– it seemed as if he could do whatever he liked, and remain well-respected by his military friends.

"Continue straight on, and I'll tell you when to turn left," Mugabo guided me into what he called the "volunteer neighborhood", a pleasantly wooded area. I turned left at his instruction and we found ourselves at the outer gate of a large and beautiful modern house.

It was probably formerly occupied by one of the great officials of the city, or an expatriate from the West... We were mesmerized by the serenity and beauty of the place. It was as if there was no war, no genocide at all.

The inner enclosure was spacious, and the garden beautiful! I chose to park under a fig tree planted by green grass. To the left was a courtyard built into the cracked plaster and gravel.

Mugabo ushered us into the house, where we were tearfully reunited with Jeanne, Mugabo's wife. Waiting with her to greet us were members of four other refugee families, also living in that majestic place.

We had never met them, but we embraced them as if they were our own precious family. We were the survivors, those who remained. There were so few of us– and so many lost.

Chapter 12
The City of Healing

"In the course of a few terrible months in 1994, 1 million people were killed in Rwanda... It was slaughter on a scale not seen since the Nazi extermination programme against the Jews. The killing rate in Rwanda was five times that achieved by the Nazis."

-"A People Betrayed" by Linda Melvern

That first evening in Byumba was one I will never forget. It was a blessed return to what felt like another lifetime– one filled with meaning, friends, and joy.

For two glorious weeks we shared that palatial home with Mugabo and other refugees. We made an excellent company; we and our new housemates– all of us shared similar sorrows and heartaches, and comforted and encouraged one another in kind.

There was Speciose, a woman who had been found alive by the Inkotanyi in the middle of a heap of dead bodies, and rescued. Vedaste, isolated and bedridden with malaria, whose hope of recovery was slim. His pregnant wife his and sister-in-law, who slept in the living room with two other young ladies, on floor mats. There was Ignace, his wife, and their two-year-old son and newborn baby, who shared a room with their housekeeper. And Mugabo Jean, his wife Jeanne, and sister Revocate, who roomed next to us, among others. All of them were broken by the horrors of the last month, and all of them had come together for healing.

We enjoyed peaceful showers, hearty meals, and relaxing conversations. There were gardens with vegetables and fruits, and chickens and cows on the grounds. We feasted on omelets and fresh fruit in the mornings. Soldiers and new neighbors came to visit, curious to hear Jeanne and I tell our remarkable story. Byumba was by far the finest of havens for genocide survivors, and we, in our grand and well-supplied house, were among the most fortunate refugees in Byumba.

We still had the Peugeot 305 with us, the gift of the FPR that I'd risked so much to acquire. On most days I visited at least one of the other refugee centers in the city, scouring them for any of our friends or family members who might have survived. I found one friend, Kayitare, who had narrowly escaped the massacres with his family.

I was also reunited with a cousin of mine, Marie. Her husband was dead, and all of her children dead but one. Her countenance, once famously cheerful, was now weary and haggard, the outward symbol of a soul forever changed by the triumph of evil. She also took shelter there, in the city of healing.

Most surprising of all, I met our friend Protogène in Byumba. I had last seen him waiting helplessly with me in my own home as the Interahamwe blasted their way inside. Frozen by fear, he had refused to make a run for it with me, instead finding a hiding place inside the ceiling. We were both delighted to now see one another, and spent an afternoon sharing our respective tales of survival.

Proto could tell us nothing about whether our beloved Josias, Yvette, or Higiro had lived or died. He had gone uncaptured by the militia in that first attack, remaining hidden in his cramped space below the roof until the soldiers and thugs and wandered off late at night. He, like us, had attempted to sneak past the Interahamwe and reach an FPR-controlled position, but had been caught crossing one of the roadblocks. They had beaten him within an inch of his life, and left him for dead.

Protogène had the Interahamwe's recklessness and lack of thoroughness to thank for his narrow escape. The drunken killers had left his head and chest gashed open, but his life still within him. Late at night he had crawled the rest of the distance to safety, and been directly borne away to Byumba, for medical attention.

It was here in Byumba that I first felt what is commonly called "survivor's guilt." I was impatient to see my children, who were no doubt safe and waiting for us in Kenya, but did not dare speak about them publicly, among so many who had lost sons and daughters. I thankfully embraced my wife every evening, surrounded by those who had seen their husbands or wives hacked to pieces and left without a burial. Why had God been so merciful to us, among so many more worthy? I could not guess at the reason, but resolved that I would find the purpose for which we had been saved, and fulfill it.

I visited the Byumba hospital from time to time. The seriously injured and sick were there, and misery beyond comprehension. A woman and child pulled half-dead from a deep pit filled with ammonia and garbage. A survivor covered in machete wounds, who had lost her fingers grabbing defensively at a knife that would have stabbed her belly. Girls raped repeatedly and left alone to die in the fields. It was unimaginable horror– enough to make one doubt the very existence a God of immeasurable love, who made Man in His own image.

Yet in this hellish environment I also saw selflessness, sacrifice, and caring. My heart is still moved by the memory of the medical workers, so many of them volunteers, diligently doing all that they could to heal and comfort the helpless. They came on behalf of Doctors Without Borders, the Salvation Army, and other charities, from both within and outside Rwanda. There was beauty to be seen in the Byumba hospital, among the ashes of mankind's very worst deeds.

We heard that the fighting in Kigali, the capital, had escalated, and that the Rwandan Armed Forces were close to retreating for good. With more and more territory being captured by the FPR, it looked as if the genocide would soon be over as well.

The soldiers spoke about one area after another being "cleared" of what they often called "the Hutu threat." But I heard nothing of Hutu innocents like Gaetan in the rebels' stories of victory. It seemed as if no Hutu civilian had been found anywhere.

Any Hutu with common sense would flee before the arrival of the FPR. So perhaps there would be none for the rebels to find and protect. But where could they have fled? Was there a safe place for Gaetan to escape to? Politically moderate Hutus– ministers, and others not considered "loyal" enough to the Interahamwe cause– had commonly been victims of the genocide, but there were few such Hutu to be found among the survivors in Byumba. For that matter, where were the Hutu native to Byumba? Not a single house or apartment in the city was occupied by its original owner. None of the refugees that I met seemed to be native to the area. I began to understand why the entire city could be handed over so completely to FPR authority. Byumba had been "cleared."

Jean Mugabo, only days after we'd arrived, even offered me a rifle and invited me to go "rooting" through Kigali with him, looking for valuables among the abandoned neighborhoods taken by the Inkotanyi. I declined his offer as skillfully as I could, making one excuse after another until he gave up the attempt and took off with his army companions, leaving me in peace.

New refugees continued to come pouring into the city. And curiously, many departed as well– abruptly, and without explanation. A family would suddenly be missing their father. Other times, entire households vanished. It was almost always the Hutu refugees, or those of mixed ancestry, who went missing. Wild rumors spread of secret hearings and refugees suspected of being spies or Interahamwe conspirators. The gossip set every survivor on edge for fear that the enemy might still be lurking among us. But no one dared to question the FPR for details about these secret matters. In spite of my fame and good reputation among the survivors, even I felt a twinge of fear. My birth certificate and national ID both described me as Hutu. I did not believe that I would be suspected as one of these traitors and spies, but I dared not call attention to myself either.

It was this unspoken fear of our own protectors that gripped my heart on what was about the fifth day in the camp, when I returned home in the evening to find an imposingly large, camouflaged pickup truck parked beside my own car.

It belonged to Afande Rukoko, a man known and feared throughout Byumba. He was the manager of the entire city of refugees, and the commander of the rebel forces here.

I had crossed his path a few times before, while driving in town, and his icy stare had always set me on edge.

I acted as casually as I could coming through the door, greeting my housemates who were seated around the table. Mugabo was not with us; he had been gone already for two days, still looting the city of Kigali. How I longed for his calming presence when I saw the sour-faced Afande seated at the table as a guest!

Jeanne was present, and introduced us after a moment of awkward silence.

"Afande, this is my husband Charles."

The officer seemed bored already with small-talk. We shook hands and exchanged the most common and polite salutations.

"Pleased to meet you, Charles. How are you?"

"I am fine, Afande, thank you."

He rose and stretched himself. There were two other men, in civilian clothes, seated with him.

"We are the policy framers of the FPR in this city," he spoke directly to me, "and we have come to tell you that we want that Peugeot car. We will take the keys now."

I offered them willingly. "I am happy to give it to you. I got it from the FPR to begin with, and I can get along fine without it. Please take it tonight with my compliments."

His expression did not change. "You will be working for us as well. We need a skilled driver, and we don't want to spare any trained soldiers for such work."

Had this request come from anyone else, I might have protested. But Afande Rokoko could not be denied; his word was the law in Byumba.

Jeanne could not hide her surprise and horror at my unwelcome recruitment, and apparently neither could I, as the Afande seemed to read my expression.

"You can continue to live here. But you must be available at all times when we call for you. Sometimes you will work here in the city, and sometimes you will go with the troops on a mission. Good night."

I wished more than anything that Mugabo were there at the house. Perhaps he could have intervened. As it was, the Afande, a man accustomed to having his orders obeyed, excused himself without another word.

That night I tried my best to console my sleepless wife. We had endured so much at one another's side– it was unthinkable that I could be placed in danger again by the very forces who had rescued us from hell! She could not bear the thought of me dying apart from her. I shared her fears, but put on a bold front for her; assuring her that a driver's work was not so great risk, that most of the danger from the FAR was past, and even that we might be paid some money for our troubles.

Today, I do not regret being pressed into this service. There was a sort of providence to it, in fact. It allowed me to be an eyewitness to new revelations; hidden ones, of which I cannot now speak openly.

From that day forward, I drove nearly every day in the service of the Patriotic Forces of Rwanda.

I would often shuttle important people from Byumba to Mulindi, the headquarters of the FPR high command. Sometimes I would drive to the orphanages of Tare and Ngarama. Officers and party politicians occasionally needed a ride while on business in Byumba. Occasionally I would take part in the night patrols of the Military Police, helping them track down soldiers who had deserted their barracks looking for women.

There was nothing particularly life-threatening about most of these missions. But they were unpleasant to me– especially being compelled to hear the soldiers' casual accounts of the Hutus they had killed. It made me endlessly nervous around the officers, afraid of falling out of their favor, or even being suspected as a Hutu spy. It was an irrational fear, perhaps, but it was fed by the daily sight of other Hutu civilians arrested for their apparent role in the

231

massacres. The Inkotanyi were efficient to a degree that seemed impossible when it came to catching and prosecuting Hutu citizens who had taken some role or another in assisting the genocide; as illogical as it seemed, it chilled my blood to see it. You can imagine, then, how I was actually quite relieved to one day awaken feeling terribly sick, and no longer able to fulfill my duties.

I was forced to stay home and rest until a full recovery was made. The Rwandan nurse working for Doctors Without Borders suspected I was coming down with malaria, and proscribed medicines. For three days I was bedridden– in pain, but free from my tiresome duties as a driver, at least for a while.

The day came when I began to feel well again, able to eat properly and walk around the house. That fateful morning I was visited by Afande Aaron, the second-in-command to Rukoko.

Unlike his superior, Aaron was personable and seemed to have taken a liking to me after first hearing my story. I considered him a friend, and was not surprised to see him approach our house. He had visited us three days before, to check on my health when I'd first fallen sick.

There was a different feel to today's visit. Two more officers were with him, and the three of them came in all at once, and asked whether they could meet with me privately. Once more my heart quickened, as it had on the night when I'd first been recruited to drive. *Had they discovered my official ethnicity? Were they going to question me?*

They escorted me some distance away from the house, where Afande Aaron did all the talking.

"Mr. Charles, I know you well enough that I believe I can trust you. I would like you to work with me in some military operations. I am counting on you, as a fellow Rwandan, to do your duty."

"What could I possibly do for you, Afande?"

232

"We know that there are undesirable elements mixed in among these refugees. Hutus. We have to screen them; find out who they are. And we have to secretly deal with them."

My apprehension at this must have been noticed, because his voice lowered and became all the more earnest.

"Charles," he entreated, "we have no choice. These volunteers and foreigners are all over the place now. A lot of them are the fanatical religious type. They don't understand anything about what's necessary to keep this place safe. They can't find out about this."

He pressed on, his passion heightening. "The United Nations is sending aid workers now. They know that the fight is almost over. They didn't do anything to stop this genocide. They want to cover their asses now. Pretend to care. So what will happen if hundreds of foreigners come into these camps? We won't be able to do as we like. We will have lost our chance to end the Hutu threat for good. Those Interahamwe monsters will escape free and clear. You *know* what they are capable of. You know more than anyone! Now is our only chance to finish it."

I concealed my revulsion. My experience as a driver had already taught me that there was truth to the rumors whispered throughout the camps; that secret operations were continuously underway to punish supposed spies and abettors of the Interahamwe hiding in the camps, of whom, we were meant to believe, there were hundreds at least.
"Are there really Interahamwe around here? Among the refugees?" I feigned surprise.

He looked sternly at me. "Why Charles, you know there are. And you will recognize them. You must help us identify them."

I regret to say that I cannot reveal any more, at present, about what followed; about my miserable final week in the city of healing. I have written several pages' worth about the days after that conversation with Afande Aaron– and I am forced to withhold those pages, for the sake of a great many innocent people's safety.

Those suppressed pages– containing the story of the second half of our stay in Byumba– remain with me. And it is my hope that someday soon I will be at liberty to share them, perhaps in a second book. Only know that our first week in Byumba was all heavenly, blissful ignorance– and the second week a waking nightmare. I saw things, during those last seven days, which anguish my heart to think upon, even to this day. I lost many of my delusions that week. More I cannot say, except that I have two comforts in the presence of those awful memories: that I myself survived, and that my conscience remains clear.

It was late in the evening– one night before the war for Rwanda officially ended. Our last night spent in Byumba.

I was taxied home once more by an officer of the Rwandan Patriotic Army; I no longer served as a driver for them, and had no car of my own. Inside, all of our housemates were sound asleep. I curled up beside a sleeping Jeanne, buried my face beneath my arm, and shut my eyes, a thoroughly broken spirit. She stirred next to me.

"Why did they keep you so late, dear? What did you do today?"

As it had been the previous few days, I could say nothing. Neither could I cry, or sleep, or feel.

Chapter 13
Magayane

"I think the [Clinton] administration did the right thing in that case...It was a horrible situation. No one liked to see it on our TV screens, but it's a case where we need to make sure we've got an early warning system...And so I thought they made the right decision not to send U.S. troops into Rwanda."

-U.S. President George W. Bush
October 2000

On July 4th, 1994, the city of Byumba erupted into celebration. The war was officially ended, the FAR were defeated, and the entire capital city of Kigali was finally under the control of the Rwandan Patriotic Front. There was leaping and shouting in the streets.

I traveled with Jean Mugabo in his own car to Kigali– we wanted to tour the city, to make certain that it was safe to resettle there with our families. We would have to find ourselves new places to live before coming back to Byumba for our loved ones.

The city was filled with decaying bodies, gradually being burned or buried by the returning populace. It wasn't easy to feel at ease anymore in this place, the very scene of so many cold-blooded murders. And yet, there were our fellow Tutsis in the fields and streets, grieving and rejoicing, setting out to rebuild their shattered lives, and walking about free of fear.

There is a recent legend in Rwanda, springing forth from a mysterious man, a wanderer, who came from the north some forty years ago. He was Magayane– regarded by many as a prophet; a seer. The story goes that he was once brought before President Habyarimana, where he predicted the rise to power and eventual death of the man whose assassination would be the beginning of our land's ruin.

Rwandans latched on to one particular phrase of the lengthy Magayane prophesy: that "the country will eventually know real joy, peace, and riches." It took on a larger meaning to them, this vision of blessing and contentment– to the point that the name *Magayane* came to signify the hope of national prosperity.

It was this prosperity that the returning genocide survivors from Kigali believed themselves to be experiencing as they arrived, mourning and penniless, back in their old neighborhoods. Any reasonable soul coming back to build a life in such a ruined place could expect, at least, years of scarcity and hardship. And so it should come as a great

236

surprise that the wonders that greeted us in Kigali brought the cry of "Magayane!" to so many lips.

Nearly every house still standing was uninhabited! There were precious few Tutsi survivors. The remaining Interahamwe had fled the city, as had all Hutus not still among the refugees. The wealthiest citizens, in particular, had long since fled, with only what they could carry.

Vehicles were abandoned everywhere. If you could get your hands on the keys, any car could be yours. Every survivor who wished for a car or truck soon had one. It was the same for houses, television sets, refrigerators, and furniture. Families lustily staked their claim on empty homes, larger and more luxurious homes than anything they had known before.

To be sure, there was a squabble or two over choice properties, but for the most part, there were far too many spoils, and too few survivors to claim them! The soldiers and police had set aside the best for themselves, and still there was too much. They came in their largest trucks, delivering furniture and appliances from storage to any Tutsi who asked. No one lacked anything they desired.

"It is the fulfillment of the prophesy of Magayane!" So it was said among the excited people. They were receiving their well-deserved compensation for their suffering.

"Magayane" became more than a mere name. It was a state of euphoria. This was Magayane. From now on, Magayane was the bright future for Rwanda's oppressed. Prosperity. Comfort. It was difficult to remain bad-tempered when any material thing you'd ever wanted was suddenly yours for the taking.

I myself could not share so much in the enthusiasm of the crowd, and not for lack of trying. My joy was tempered, and my heart still heavy, by the memory of what I'd seen in secret, in Byumba. Side by side with my old friend Mugabo, I marveled at the riches that now belonged to our fellow refugees. But I knew whose property much of it had been.

There were new UNAMIR forces in the city now, troops from Ghana, overseeing and controlling the area in conjunction with the FPR. They were comically late to the genocide, but eager to help in the resettling efforts. They saluted us, and instructed Mugabo and I, just as they had the others returning from exile. We were welcome to search for any house that met our needs, and occupy it, provided that it was not already claimed.

"My friend Charles here," Mugabo boisterously addressed a pair of them, "has no car of his own. His wife is in Byumba, and he must return to bring her here. They have three children in Kenya, waiting to come home to their…"

Without waiting to hear another word, one of the Ghanaians handed me the keys to a Volkswagen Kombi, in excellent condition. Just like that!

We returned to Kimironko, my old neighborhood, where the wreckage of my house lay. It was a surreal thing, you can imagine, surveying in daylight the places where we had been trapped and hunted like wild beasts by night. We were both looking for new homes for our families, but I was also eager to see the Biramvu residence, and especially Gaetan's house. I wanted to be sure that they were still alive and safe. I stopped at both places, only to find them boarded up and empty. Dr. Alphonse and his family, I knew, had fled Kigali soon after the killings had begun. It looked as if Gaetan had eventually done the same. There were only a few homes nearby not torn to shreds, looted, and wrecked. Of those still inhabitable, a mere handful were occupied, and no one could tell me what had become of either Dr. Alphonse or Gaetan.

Could Gaetan, his wife, and children be in refugee camps? Had they fled towards Congo? *It is too early*, I thought, *for most people from Kigali to return to their homes. Especially Hutu people. They might be waiting until they're sure it's safe...*My heart would not allow me to think that they had come to harm.

Mugabo and I separated for a while. I drove up to a cluster of empty houses to look them over. As I exited the car, a senior officer of the FPR hailed me.

"Are you having any trouble, sir? You look distressed."

He had seen that I was driving a military-colored car, and suspected that I was myself a soldier. I respectfully greeted him.

"I am one of the survivors of the genocide. I just came from Byumba. My home was destroyed, and I am looking for a new place to house my family."

"Well you're in luck! I just moved from that house."

He pointed to a large property concealed by a gated brick wall. Two trucks were parked outside, armed soldiers at the wheel.

"If you like it, it's all yours. Everything you need is inside. Here."

He tossed me the iron keys to the gate, as casually as if I had asked him for a cigarette.

"Thank you, Afande..." I was quite taken aback by all of this. "I'm really honored to have met you today. It means so much to my family and I..."

He was already jogging back to meet his escort by the gate. I waved gratefully, waiting until they had driven away before having a look at the estate that had apparently just become my own.

I would never have even considered such a place had it not been offered me! It was far too large for us, even with the children. There were eight bedrooms, a dresser in each. Two separate living rooms, both with luxurious furniture: chairs and leather sofas, bookshelves, a television and home theater. There was a very modern L-shaped kitchen, with a large American refrigerator and double sink.

I walked out into the backyard, which was beautiful with fruit trees and outdoor quarters for the use of a cook.

Back inside I found a laundry room with an unused washing machine and dryer. I had always considered myself well-off, but had never owned such things before.

It was hard to resist getting caught up in some of the same euphoria that had fully captured so many other displaced Kigalians. *Magayane!* Our children would soon return to us, and we would live at peace in this magnificent place...

Across the street was an attractive smaller house that seemed deserted as well. I wondered if Protogene would like to live there. We could be neighbors again.

I rejoined Mugabo as planned as planned for the journey back to Byumba. It was late in the evening by the time we arrived there. The camp was bustling with excited Tutsi refugees packing and preparing for their journeys home. They were even bursting into song:

> *Freedom–*
> *Every man for himself to another life,*
> *Every man for himself to another destiny!*

It was the illusion of Magayane, the mysterious prophet.

Mugabo had been chosen to live in an exclusive and wealthy neighborhood, set aside for senior officials, diplomats and the like. We bid a fond farewell to him and to the other refugees with whom we had shared those pleasant quarters for so long. We all exchanged information that night and the following morning, promising to try and contact one another when we could.

I was excited to show Jeanne our new car, and tell her all about the splendid home I had been given near our old neighborhood. It was so large, I told her, that we would feel quite lonely there by ourselves. And so we asked Revocate, Mugabo's sister, if she would come join us there, and she wholeheartedly accepted.

Jeanne and I were no longer hesitant to dream out loud about our plans to reunite with the children. We would arrange for their uncle to bring them. Everything was nearly ready.

Our new home was near the IAMSEA Institute, which had been converted into an FPR military barracks. It was a safe place to live, as we gained the acquaintance of many of the soldiers, and they provided security for us. As it had been everywhere else, many of them asked us to share our remarkable story. Some of them asked us to bring them on a tour of the wreckage of our old house, and to see the place where we had hidden underground. I began to dread these visits from the soldiers, reliving in my mind the death of Vianey Biramvu, as told to us by his brother Deo…the cruel rejection by our minister friend Franco…They were unpleasant memories, all, and the sweetest of them, those of the Hutu friends who had sheltered and protected us, were spoiled by the nagging worry; the sight of their still-empty houses.

The tales of our adventures would always end with our rescue by the FPR, and the weeks spent in Byumba. The memories of Byumba were especially hurtful to me.

Citizens that had avoided the genocide, and their relatives that fled the country before the horrors, were now returning. The number of triumphant returnees grew, but Kigali never seemed to run out of abandoned properties. The new opulence was staggering; it felt like magic. Everywhere "Magayane" was sung in the praises of the people. There was no need to work, little or no state leadership. Everyone divided the spoils. The prophesy had come true, or so it seemed.

The FPR continued to make certain their victory. For those Hutus who had no part in the bloodshed, hoping to return in peace to their homes, there was no *Magayane*. They were foreign to the common interest, despised and resented, and treated roughly by civilians and soldiers alike. Their insistence upon their human rights was a bucket of cold water; an infringement upon the fulfillment on the wonderful prophesies. They often fled, or rather disappeared; and those who remained lived in continual fear. The Inkotanyi, now agents of the new transitional government, still spoke of "clearings" and "sweepings".

UNAMIR contributed significantly to the cleanup and reconstruction efforts. Businesses appeared from abroad. Products and services slowly returned. Football and volleyball games were organized. There was reality to be rejoined, and normalcy to be gradually restored.

Squabbles arose too– between native Rwandans and exiles who had been living in neighboring countries; between survivors bickering over property; and between the military and a population that was becoming harder to control. The jovial, brotherly nature of our relationships with the Inkotanyi slowly gave way to tension. They were no longer so friendly towards civilians. We gradually came to accept this, and were content just to keep out of their way.

Jeanne and I, one wonderful day, at last had the opportunity to reach our brother on the telephone. We rejoiced to hear our children's voices; to assure them that we were alive and would soon see and touch them. We insisted that they come home quickly, without delay.

There were difficulties in arranging their trip, and in transporting them across the national border. In the meantime, in October of 1994, I began work again, in the field of customs declaration. It was a well-paying job for the time, and I was happy to have the means to provide for our family, soon to be reunited. Our cavernous, barren new home would soon be filled with the voices of children. My in-laws and other living relatives, who had believed us dead, came rejoicing, handling us as if we were spirits returned from heaven. We were content.

I had a daily routine again, with responsibilities, as before. I was able to think less about the nightmares in our recent past, and the hurtful and precious memories of my beloved, lost brothers Guillaume and Benoit. Work kept my mind on other things.

And soon afterwards came the day when our little ones, Yves, Luke, and Lyndz, came running across the front lawn to meet us! I was as happy on that tearful morning as I have ever been before or since. It was a more wonderful day than it had been in my dreams, when lying exhausted inside that earthen pit I had found my strength by imagining this very moment!

They had already grown so much taller! And they spoke like true Kenyans, in Swahili and in proper English.

I took tiny Lyndz in my arms, thanking God for giving us the presence of mind to have sent them safely away long before the genocide. For giving us the mercy and courage to have hidden and survived for weeks on end. For sustaining us with His voice in those darkest hours. I didn't deserve any of it. I'd never been any sort of saint. I would never forget it.

The anticipation of that glorious day had kept us alive as we sat in the shadow of death. And the memory of it would do the same, in equally dark days still to come.

The children were ecstatic about their new home, with its lawn and gardens. They took frequent trips to the wreckage of our old place, looking for relics of their former life to triumphantly bring back to us. They even recovered a handful of wrinkled pages from our old photo albums.

Then came another joyful reunion, with the return of Dr. Alphonse Biramvu and his wife Verene, whose son Vianey had died defending us from the militias. Their family was among those brave Hutu who came back from exile, guiltless of the massacres, to live among their Tutsi brothers in their own original homes. But they did not all return.

Their youngest son, the bold and handsome Deo, was gone. It was Deo who had kept us company in his family's home, sheltering us from his fellow Hutus drunk with hatred. He had risked his life for me a second time, on the day that his brother Vianey was murdered. But it was not because of the genocide that this worthy hero had now died.

Deo had been killed quite recently, traveling to his hometown of Cyangugu to accompany his parents back to Kigali. The FPR had arrested him, mistakenly accusing him of committing acts of genocide, over his mother and father's protests. He was taken away, never to be seen again.

Dr. Biramvu had always been greatly respected, by Hutu and Tutsi alike, for his character and kindness to all. But no more. His revered status in the community was gone. In the new Kigali the good doctor's lack of prejudice was no longer remembered. He was, like all so-called 'Hutu' here, a living symbol of the miseries that had befallen the Tutsi, and subject to a great deal of prejudice and harsh treatment.

It was my opportunity to repay some small measure of Christian kindness to him. I visited the house almost daily, where I had once taken shelter as the FAR troops ransacked my home, hunting for us. I took care to spread the word to every neighbor, officer of the FPR, and anyone else who would listen that the Biramvu family ought to be considered national heroes. I never once shared my own story without also recounting in detail how Verene and Alphonse had risked all– and lost their son– to save us. They became an uncle and auntie to our children, and on our frequent visits to their home we made sure that they were comfortable and unmolested.

During one such visit with Dr. Alphonse, I found myself, as I often did, looking in the direction of Gaetan's place, wherein we had endured so much danger. From

Alphonse's veranda I could see the wreckage of my former house and car, still not cleared away, and not far from there was the neglected old house of Gaetan, and the field where there had once been banana trees. The pit in which I had lived for weeks was still nearby, now filled with debris and dirt. No one had yet wanted to claim the slumping, boarded-up house, and I passed it regularly while driving, in hopes that Gaetan, Dianne, and their children might have returned home.

On this day my heart leapt out of my chest. I had given up on the hope of ever seeing Gaetan again, or even knowing what had become of him. But there in the yard was Dianne heading out of the front door to fetch water, a plastic jerry-can in her right hand, and her toddler clinging to her back! I rushed towards her, both excited and nervous. It was unmistakably her, our angel.

She was forlorn and thoughtful, and did not lift her head and recognize me until we were standing face to face. Her mouth dropped open at the sight of me, alive.

"Am I dreaming...or is it you, Papa Yves?" (She addressed me according to the Rwandan custom of calling a father after the name of his first-born.)

"It is me...Charles." I was overcome by emotion. "I am glad to have lived to see you and your family again. We have never forgotten you."

I couldn't help but notice that she had become haggard and disturbingly thin. Her cheekbones protruded.

"Dianne, is your husband here? Dianne...Madame?" Her countenance changed. She looked straight ahead, as if at something far beyond me. I had sent her to a horrible place. *Could it possibly be that Gaetan...*

"Madame, I am sorry. Has something happened? Please...I hope there isn't any bad news. Forgive me..."

She turned away and burst into tears for a full half-minute. When she could finally speak, it was only through sobs.

"My husband...was killed. They–

245

"Killed? By whom?" My voice was cracking as well. I grew heartbroken and furious all at once. Surely he had died because of us! The Interahamwe must have come for him, just as his nephew Modesto had threatened.

The lump in my throat grew at the thought of it. "You mean Modesto…the Interahamwe…"

"No!" She had crumpled to the ground with the child tightly in her arms, weeping softly. "He was killed by the Inkotanyi!"

My own strength left me. I fell to the grass and sat, crying along with her. Few of the things I had seen this awful year could have ruined me like this! *Gaetan, dead, at the hands of the FPR? The ones who had saved my life had also taken his? How could such a mistake have been made?*

"Oh, sister…it can't be…they didn't know about what you did for us? Did you try to tell them? Don't they know that you are not Interahamwe?"

"He…tried to tell them. We begged them. We told them…that his brother Fidel was even in their army…Gaetan…wanted them to contact him, to prove his innocence, but they wouldn't allow it…they killed him!"

So it was then. I cursed myself for ever idolizing them! They would take in and recruit a boy to fight for them, and kill his brother who had delivered him to them in safety!

She was doubled over the child now, rocking and sobbing. I longed to say something to comfort her.

"Madame…I am so sorry. He was a godly man. A good man. I…never met a better soul than him. We will see him again."

This had some small effect.

"Please tell me," I continued. "Your other children. They are safe?"

"Yes, we are all here. But my oldest daughter is very sick…maybe malaria."

I wiped my face with my sleeve and helped the grieving lady back to her feet. I searched my pockets and drew out all of the money therein.

246

"Please take it. It's all I have with me. When you go for water you can buy medicine tonight. We will both come to see you first thing tomorrow morning. From now on, you are family to us, sister."

She composed herself, received my humble gift, and picked up the tiny child again. "Thank you. God bless you." I had turned to go.

"Charles."

"Yes?"

"You said 'we'...then your wife is with you?"

"Yes, sister. She is very well, and our children are here with us."

She thought about this for a moment. Her careworn face produced something rather like a smile.

"I am glad."

As we both returned to go about our own business, I understood that our own survival and happiness had done more for the poor widow than any of my awkward attempts at speaking comfort. She was certain that her husband's bravery had made an important difference in this lost and dying world.

Gaetan and Doctor Alphonse, by all rights, should be recognized for generations to come as national heroes. Their names deserve eternal respect among Rwandans, all Africans, and any of God's children who love unity and brotherhood. Instead, their story remains untold and their heroism remains forever unrecognized.

Many of the true heroes and saints of 1994 will go without the fame that they deserve, until that final Day when all is known and nothing can be hidden. While many murderers, no doubt, received, and still receive, the highest of honors.

Chapter 14
Underground Again

"The world must deeply repent this failure. Rwanda's tragedy was the world's tragedy. All of us who cared about Rwanda, all of us who witnessed its suffering, fervently wish that we could have prevented the genocide."
-U.N. Secretary-General Kofi Annan
May 7, 1998

"They were running towards us with guns. Once we heard the firing, we panicked. We ran out of the house, people were running away everywhere. We got lost in the crowd…"

My late brother's widow had come to visit us. We were home from church, and she was telling the story of how she and her children had survived the genocide. Seated nearby was my cousin Gemima, who had watched her own sons and daughters killed in front of her. It was a somber reunion.

"I had Sheja with me, and Guillaume had the boys. We were separated from each other in the mob of people running. I didn't see him anywhere. People were falling down, shot.

"I don't look like a Tutsi, so I covered Sheja's face as much as I could and tried to get out of the crowd. I wanted to leave Kabeza, to get somewhere where we'd be safe. I told everyone at the roadblocks that we were Hutu.

"Then I heard that the Colonel, Nsekarije, had a compound not far away. I didn't know if it was safe there, but I remembered hearing that he loved the Tutsi people and that he had resigned from the army for reasons of conscience…I heard that refugees were running and hiding there, so that's where we went. They welcomed us…we stayed there for three months…

"I never heard any news about Guillaume…I didn't know until after the war that he was dead…"

She had begun to weep, and my wife wept with her. Little Lyndz, our youngest, had grown bored with watching her brothers play video games, and wandered in from the living room. She was listening to us intently. Seeing her mother cry, she began to cry, too.

"There will never be anyone like our Guillaume," I offered. I wanted our memories of him to be happy ones, and not painful thoughts about his execution by militias. "His humor…his love of music. He taught me how to play guitar. He loved the old songs..."

My voice trailed away. "He wanted to make sure that they were never forgotten…"

My wife and sister-in-law recovered themselves, but tiny Lyndz was now both sobbing and shaking. I swept her into my arms and carried her to her room, whispering soothingly to her. She had reached the age at which children ask endless questions.

"Dad," she sprang up as soon as I'd lain her on the bed, "why did they kill Papa Minou and Uncle Benoit?"

I didn't have a ready response. How can a child understand such things?

She persisted. "Dad, if we hadn't gone away, were they going to kill us too, like my cousins?"

I stroked her hair. "It's true dear, they killed Papa Minou and the others. But they all went to heaven. They're with God now, so they are at peace and don't have anything to worry about anymore."

She gave my answer some thought.

"If they are in heaven then why didn't you and Mama want to go too? And why didn't you let us all go?"

Well, now I'd made a mess of things. So the Interahamwe were leading people to heaven! I wished I had let Jeanne handle this discussion. She always seemed to know the right things to say.

"My dear Lyndz, God gave us this life. He can take people to heaven if he wants to. But we cannot decide when it's time to go to heaven. And to take someone else's life is murder. It is a sin. What those men did to your uncles was evil, even if it caused them to go to heaven. They could have had a longer life and helped a lot more other people if they hadn't been…killed."

I thought that I was making sense of things for myself as much as for her.

She seemed pleased enough with this answer, and eager to take advantage of my thoughtful mood.

"And is it a sin to be a Tutsi?"

Jeanne had come into the room and was watching us. She might have been curious about how I would handle this new line of questioning.

"No, of course not. To be Tutsi means nothing. Some people are tall. Some are short. Some people have dark skin, and some have light skin. Some people look like Tutsi and some look like Hutu. It doesn't matter. Everyone is a person. God made all of us."

"Then why did they try to kill all of the Tutsi?"

Now there was an excellent question! The right response would have to be a lengthy and confusing one, I thought. Historical grievances? Political ideologies? Economic inequality? The psychology behind racism and tribal identity?

"Because, darling, they are all fools. Good night."

It was April 8th, 1995.

It had been a full year.

I drove out through our front gate after giving a few instructions to the children. We were temporarily without electricity in our area, as often happened, and we needed to take special precautions for safety's sake.

Not much had changed in the city. There was little talk of Magayane anymore.

My cousin and sister-in-law were still with us. A friend of ours named Kamado, a soldier in the new Rwandan military, had been visiting at our home as well. I had offered to drop all three of them off that Sunday afternoon: to a prayer meeting, home, and a friend's house, respectively. Our route happened to take us past the entrance to the National Stadium, the very place where the FPR forces had once saved our lives.

As we drove past the Stadium, I noticed a white car following close behind me, without a license-plate number and with windows tinted black. I recognized it as one of the vehicles driven by military intelligence– the DMI.

He passed me and pulled in front, signaling for me to pull over with his hands.

This was no routine traffic-stop. An intelligence officer would not have hailed us unless it was on serious business. I was frightened, and thankful to have Kamado with me.

Obediently, I slowed and stopped, noticing that there were two uniformed soldiers inside carrying the standard Kalashnikov rifles.

My heart was already pounding. What could they want from me? If their intentions were friendly, then why not a simple phone call?

"These are DMI agents. What do they want?" Kamado questioned me.

"I can't imagine. Maybe they have something to ask you?"

"Perhaps they confused this car with someone else's."

"It's possible. An officer gave it to me."

We had convinced ourselves to hope for the best by the time both of the officers approached us on foot, on my side. I rolled down the window, and they took a long look at the four of us.

They greeted us, and asked our names. I was happy to learn that one of them was familiar with Kamado.

Kamado and the officer made uncomfortable small talk for a moment.

"Sir," I needed my fears assuaged. "May I ask you why it is that you stopped us?"

"Do you know Mr. Kamado?" He questioned back.

"Afande, do you know this guy?" the other officer asked Kamado, without waiting for an answer from me.

"This gentleman and his family are my neighbors. His name is Charles, he's a friend."

"Yes, I am Charles. Is there something you wanted to tell me, Afande?"

"It's nothing serious sir. We only have a few simple questions for you."

If only that could be true! I tested it immediately.

"Of course Afande, and if you like I can step out of the car and we can walk over there and speak in private…"

"No," he shook his head, "we will not talk here on the road. I must ask you to come in to the office."

Then this questioning, whatever it is, could take a very long time. Surely I am not in any kind of trouble? My expression hardly changed, but I was now far beyond frightened. Always, lurking in the back of my mind, had been the fear that my mixed heritage as a "Hutsi" would create problems for us in the new government. I had always suppressed these fears as unreasonable…

I did my best to appear calm. "Gentlemen, I am running a lot of errands this afternoon, and taking these good people home. Would it be possible for me to come to see you tomorrow, in the morning?

He lost the polite veneer. "You think I have time to waste waiting for you to run around? Get out of the car. Your passengers can drive it home or go on foot. You have to come in to the office. Those are my orders."

"Don't argue with them," whispered Kamado. "This is serious. If they are going to arrest you, I can't do anything about it now. They only answer to their boss."

Arrest me! As it began to sink in, my heart fell. My cousin and sister quietly wondered what could possibly be going on.

"Sir…" in spite of Kamado, I was simply not willing to be carried away to God-knows-where with no warning. "This is really an unusual situation. At least let me drop off my friends and then I will report to your office right away. Or else tell me, is this an arrest? What is happening?"

Kamado chimed in and assured them both that he would make sure to take me to the Intelligence offices himself after the ladies were dropped off.

Perhaps because Kamado technically outranked them, the two officers saluted him and allowed my request. I was to report to the DMI offices in Kimihurura, within an hour.

This small victory was helpful, I thought. I now had a brief window of time with which to contact every powerful person I could, to tell them of my situation. Secretly I feared the worst, remembering what had happened to Gaetan and to Deo, and aware that I had continually praised both to whomever would listen…if the FPR really thought that those two had been criminals, than what might they think of me? I was eager to get to a telephone.

But as soon as we were back on the road, it was clear that we would not be left alone. The unmarked car followed close behind us. I warned Gemima and Jeanne, my sister-in-law, that we should not speak a word.

They, like me, couldn't believe that this could happen. It was less than a year ago that I had been chased through the streets like a dog by the Hutu government. The FPR were certainly not after our lives, but the feelings of fear and intimidation rushing over me were as familiar now as before. It made me rather angry; I wondered if I could ever be allowed to live my life unmolested by authorities of some kind. I had never harmed anyone, and wanted nothing from them!

We delivered our two passengers to their destinations, as promised. Both times, the ominous white car remained directly behind us, parking alongside us as I said goodbye to first Gemima, and then Jeanne. I said nothing alarming; I did not want to frighten them by sharing my worst fears.

It was only when we were alone that Kamado spoke.

"Don't take me to my friend's house. Change of plans. We'll go to the DMI headquarters right away. I promised that I would deliver you there on time."

I was wondering if he would be willing to do anything to help me.

"You never know, he added, "I know many of them; maybe I can talk to them and do something for you. I'm not going to leave you there not knowing why they summoned you or what they're going to do."

It gave me courage to know that a military friend of some influence was already on my side. It didn't look as if I was going to have a chance to reach a phone, with our every move followed.

"Do you really think that I might be in some kind of trouble?"

"Who can tell…probably they just want to ask you some questions about some suspicious person. Don't be too worried."

I was well within my one-hour time limit when Kamado and I parked outside of the office building. The menacing white car with the tinted windows parked nearby as well.

"I truly hope that this will not take long," I hesitated to exit the car. "If it gets any later than 5 o' clock, just take this car and head home."

"And what about you?"

"I will call to arrange for a ride."

"Well good luck then, friend."

We were still willing to believe that it could all prove to be nothing.

I passed through the courtyard and into the three-story administrative building. The tall gentleman who had accosted me on the road was waiting inside, with a charming and polite smile. I was expecting to fill out all sorts of tedious paperwork upon entry, but instead he simply motioned for me to follow him.

My fear increased the deeper we marched into the belly of the place. I followed through one unadorned and unfriendly hallway after another, making noisy footsteps on the hard concrete.

The lights grew dimmer, and the hallways darker. We passed by a gigantic set of double doors that seemed important, and then around a corner, until he finally paused and drew a key-ring from his pocket. The door he selected opened into what looked like a conference room. It was filled with nothing but rows of long tables and chairs.

He preceded me inside, and then closed the door behind me. Pointing courteously to a spot in the first row of chairs, he invited me to sit. And then, without another word, he left me alone in that room. The door was shut, but not locked.

This certainly must mean that I was worrying too much. I am not being arrested. But what then? The officer must be going to bring the person who will tell me why they wanted me here... I waited there for twenty agonizing minutes.

The same tall, smiling man returned again, holding a stack of forms and blank sheets of paper. Placing them in front of me, he handed me a pen.

"These first forms are for identification. And then after that, if you could write your family history and origins, how you came to live in Kigali, and where you were before the morning of April 7th, 1994..."

This was already a sort of interrogation. I could lay to rest any hopeful thought of being brought home in time for supper. It really seemed as though they were concerned with me, and not some suspicious coworker or neighbor of mine. I couldn't think of anyone who would want to falsely accuse me for any reason. Or was I over-worrying again?

I completed the odd examination as requested, and he looked it over. Satisfied, he left me alone again, this time double-locking the door.

And now a full hour passed. It was 4:30. Then 5:30. Kamado would be gone by now. I wondered if he had learned anything about why I was here. I was checking my watch every few minutes. The sun was setting, darkening the lonely room. There was a light-switch on the wall, but it did nothing.

I began to despise that arrogant soldier for such an impolite abuse of power. There was no reason on earth to lock me in here alone without an explanation, for hours at a time! I could not fathom how the authorities could have simply forgotten me here. *We are human beings and Rwandans, like them! How can they disrespect us like this, treating us as though it is our privilege, and not our right, to walk about freely?*

I began to pace around the room, to stretch my legs. The only light now filtering in from outside was coming from street lamps. I was covered in darkness. I had been left alone for six hours now, and was convinced that I was truly under arrest, or perhaps there was a plot to kill me. My trust and admiration for the FPR was no longer what it had once been.

I began to pray, as if talking to an old friend. My emotions were boiling over, and the welcoming presence and peace of God were exactly what I most needed. My rage and panic gave way to tranquility, and determination. I would do what I could to navigate this new ordeal, but the rest was in God's hands.

It was 8 o' clock. This was normally the most precious hour of my day, surrounded by my wife and children. What were they thinking about my long absence? Jeanne would have heard about my encounter with the feared DMI, and about my appointment here. She would be frightened and worried. I was helpless to comfort her, or even to let her know that I was still alive.

I was helpless in every respect. There was no possible course of action to take. I was exhausted, and emotionally drained. I went to the corner of the room and lay down on the cold floor, looking for the most comfortable position in which to sleep.

Sleep proved impossible; I simply could not stop thinking and worrying enough to relax. I was still restlessly changing positions on the floor when a key turned in the lock on the door.

I jumped to my feet, both eager to meet someone who might assuage my doubts, and terrified of what and who might enter. The wild and horrible thought occurred to me that they might have locked me away for hours so that they could kill me more discreetly, in the middle of the night.

The newcomer was one whom I did not recognize in the darkness, but he immediately flipped the light-switch on the wall, flooding the room with a bright fluorescent glow. I had to shield my eyes at first. The electricity must have been turned off before, and then restored in the last hour.

I could see my new visitor now: a large, middle-aged, weary-looking gentleman in full uniform. A rifle was slung over his shoulder, but he did not use it. Neither did he offer an apology to me. He hardly even looked at me. He walked to the back of the room instead, and quietly began to smoke.

Other than to lift and lower his cigarette, he barely moved. I stayed still in my seat, wondering if he was under orders not to talk to me. I looked to him, making facial expressions that invited conversation. Nothing.

It was odd behavior. If I were accused as a traitor, I thought it would be typical of them to shout at me and call me all sorts of horrible names. If I were not under suspicion, they ought to have been more kind. Was it possible that this was some sort of exercise meant to break my spirit? For what purpose?

I couldn't bear the suspense any longer. I decided to take the lead and say something.

"Sir. Thank you for the light."

He hardly acknowledged me. I was not discouraged.

"Many mosquitos were bothering me, but now they are all gone, thanks to the light you have turned on."

He remained unmoved. I decided to get to the point.

"Sir, can you tell me why I am detained here?"

He glared at me venomously with bloodshot eyes.

I was frightened for a moment, but met his gaze until he turned away. I decided to continue.

"After all, I am a man like you. I have a family. I am Rwandan like you. I think I am at least entitled to know why they would lock me in here without any water or food and no bed–

"Quiet. I will not tolerate you talking to me like that, and I don't want to so much as hear the voice of an Interahamwe like you!"

For a second or two, I could only blink in silence.

"So that's it then? You are taking me for Interahamwe?"

I was not only shocked by the terrible, damning revelation, but hurt. I had never met this man, and already quite disliked him, but I was wounded to the heart to be called Interahamwe. The very word brought back memories of loved ones killed, children hacked to pieces, my wife and I hiding in outhouses from the Interahamwe and their machetes. And he sincerely believed that I was one of them! The accusation awakened a new kind of rage and pain in me. My blood boiled; I began breathing heavily.

Oh God, do not let me hate this man. He really thinks I am one of the Interahamwe…he doesn't know any better. Help me to stay calm now…

I said nothing more out loud. Certainly the FPR could not believe that I was one of the militia. This ignorant, probably illiterate soldier had been told all sorts of lies about me by others, or perhaps he only assumed that I was one of those being arrested for conspiring in the massacres. There had surely been some sort of mistake, although there was nothing to gain by trying to convince this fellow that I was no

Interahamwe. To say another word would only enrage him more. I would wait until his superiors came.

He had finished his cigarette. He walked back to the light-switch, and put us both into total darkness. I left my chair and crouched down in the corner at the end of the room, my heart beating hard and fast.

What could this mean? This new development set my nerves, already overwrought, into a full panic. *I am going to be beaten, and perhaps killed...*

I was not far wrong. A knock came at the door. Three more uniformed men entered. They turned on the lights, and dragged me out of my corner. The four of them were screaming in my face now. They slammed me against the wall. I cried out, protested, and begged them to hear me, but this only angered them more. They shouted questions at me.

Their questioning was without logic and beyond my comprehension. I was incredulous; I told them time and again that nothing they were saying made sense to me. They became all the more aggressive, striking me; shouting accusations and kicking my legs with heavy boots.

The crux of their interrogations, I began to understand, had something to do with conspiracies against the new government by the millions of Rwandan Hutus who had fled to Congo. They spoke of coordinated plans for bombings and assassinations, of messages sent between groups of Hutu in Congo and Uganda, of opposition parties plotting terrorist attacks that would kill thousands of people...

"Please, what does any of this have to do with me?"

They screamed at me to be quiet and to answer their questions. I could make no sense of it, until mention was made of a particular date, and a particular cargo truck that had entered into Rwanda from Kenya, on its way to Congo. When I asked what truck they referred to, one of them struck me across the face.

"You know what truck we mean. The one filled with weapons."

They had bullied and shouted at me for several minutes already, but for the first time, at least, I now understood some element of their questioning. As a customs declarer, I had been called to the border some time ago to on account of a large cargo truck. It was duly inspected, and cleared to cross, with all of the proper fees paid, and I had passed on this information to the security troops at the border.

I remembered the truck in question, because it had, shortly afterward, been attacked by Hutu rebels, looking to disturb the peace in the new Rwanda. They had tossed grenades at it.

"That truck. Yes I remember it, but there were no weapons. It was filled with cigarettes, and salt. It was inspected at the border."

I was immediately struck on the chin again. "Don't lie to us! The Hutu rebels are arming themselves with weapons from Congo. Tell us what you know!"

"The rebels would be the ones who bombed that truck; why don't you know this? I even heard about it on the radio. Do you think that I am one of these Interahamwe? Why would I hide some secret plan for them? I am telling you everything I know."

Their physical and verbal attacks grew fiercer, and I continued to show them, as best I could, the absurdity of their claims. I raised my voice to match the tone of their accusations. I told them about my only true experiences with the Interahamwe– running away from them for my life. I insisted upon meeting their superiors. I named every FPR official with whom I was friends, promising repercussions for this outrage. I told them of my friendship with Charles Kayonga, and warned them that he would learn of their treatment of me.

My interrogators seemed to think that if they continued bullying and hurting me, I would surely break down and confess to having some sort of inside knowledge of these rebel plots. They came in shifts. Four of them appeared every half-hour to harass, kick, and question me. I was already deprived of sleep; now my protestations were always countered by a fresh, belligerent group of soldiers. Sometimes they screamed in my face, insisting that I admit my guilt. Sometimes they sat me down and handed me the same set of papers, time after time, ordering me to write the facts for them. Time after time I gave them the same answers. But I was growing quieter, and weaker.

My anger and hatred were growing as well, towards these self-important bullies and whatever idiot superior had sent them to wring a confession out of me. I had sincerely believed that the genocide would illuminate to Rwanda the foolishness of racial and tribal hatred. I'd thought that a spiritual awakening would be in the works; that men would turn to the God who transcends politics and insists that we are all one blood. My head only months ago had been filled with dreams of revival, of leaders with some humility who would call for restraint and harmony. Instead they were already drunk with power!

For several long hours I suffered from the torture of both physical abuse and maddening, dull repetition. Some of my simple-minded inquisitors began to think, inwardly, that perhaps I was telling the truth. They didn't say as much, but they became more sympathetic towards me. A few of them started to look as though they realized they might be making an awful mistake. A few, but not all.

One of the more zealous of them harassed and infuriated me to no end by screaming repeatedly that I must tell "the truth."
We have heard all of your lies, tell the truth!
When will you give up and start to tell the truth?
We will continue until you are ready to tell the truth!

I wanted to slap him in the face, and it was the only truth I had for him.

"The truth!" I nearly spat. "What do you mean by the truth? Are you talking about the truth that you want to hear, or the truth that will hurt you?"

He answered quite calmly, "I did not ask you to speak in riddles. What I want is for you to tell me the truth that you know."

"And you want me to hold nothing back?"

"I am the one asking the questions, not you. Come on, don't test our patience. Tell the truth, and I warn you, don't tell a lie."

I had reached a boiling point from the punches, kicks and sleep deprivation.

"First of all…"

"Yes, we are listening."

"First of all, I am not afraid at all of you or your ignorant colleagues, Afande. Or anyone else."

I spat blood onto the ground that had collected in my throat after repeated blows to the face.

"The truth is that I am not the first innocent man to die in a place like this for no reason. The truth is that it doesn't matter how many times I tell you all about my life, my family, and my fight with the Interahamwe, you will not listen to me, because you are afraid. You are afraid that I am right, because that would prove that you are monsters. You have guns, you have authority, but you are still afraid."

He rushed at me, striking and kicking, stopping only when he had hurt his right wrist by an awkward punch which I had blocked, unintentionally, while protecting my face.

"Are you going to shut up now, or do you want me to break your ugly jaw?" He nursed his wrist. "What is wrong with you?"

"Nothing..." I spat again. "You've just…proved it. You can't do anything else to me."

The throbbing pain from the beatings had made a home within me by now. I was no longer in fear of it.

264

"You...you might have been a good man once. But what happened to you? You lost your soul, just like the others...You know I am not lying, but you're going to...just torture me until you get your..."truth"...

I wonder if this is how you start to become crazy, I thought. *I'm getting there now...* My head was spinning, and so was the room.

I didn't hear or feel any more questioning. It seemed that they were letting me lie there for the moment. I longed to have a glass of water or some food. I suspected that this was part of their torture as well.

My interrogator gathered himself.

"Are you aware of everything you just said, and to whom you speak?"

"I understand that...Afande."

"Then let's not have any more philosophy lessons. Let's talk instead about the subject that interests me– your accomplices. You're going to give us the truth that we're asking for, and you're going to pay for all of your crimes. That's the truth."

"I cannot do the impossible. If you want to find me guilty, do an investigation on me. See if I am lying. You deeply hurt me, Afande."

"What?"

"By comparing me to those Interahamwe. The ones who were my tormentors. Shame on you gentlemen!"

I braced myself for another flurry of punches, but it did not come.

I heard him walk over to a guard standing by the door.

"We'll leave him alone for a while. Make sure that no one bothers him."

He turned towards me. "I will see you again in the morning."

I thought of the martyr Stephen, in the Bible. *Father, help me see You now, as Stephen did... To know that You are here... to not to be angry. If I am to die, don't let me die filled with hate...*

The only remaining guard turned off the light and I spread myself out on the floor alone, already fading into unconsciousness. It was 3:35 in the morning.

I was thankful for the few hours of peace.

With all my heart I longed to sink into a deep sleep. But the cold, my wounds, and self-pitying thoughts of longing towards my family drove sleep far from me. I began to shiver. A fever took hold of me, and a headache so intense that I felt myself becoming delirious.

I am chained head to toe. Wild animals are running towards me. A man has come tell me that he has reviewed my chart, and now I am free to go home. My wife and children are in the car, waiting for me. I am chained head to toe. I am Interahamwe, as the smoking soldier said...

I don't know whether I slept or not, unable to distinguish dreams from hallucinations.

The officer returned, and lifted me to my feet. He ordered me to follow him out of the room. There was sunlight again.

I staggered behind him. He led me to a door through which daylight shined. I let myself dare to hope that I was being released.

There was some mistake. These officers thought that they had someone else. Now they are ashamed of their error...they will let me go now.

Instead we passed into a narrow alleyway and into a second building, in the back of the first.

This is Akabindi. No! They certainly cannot be taking me there!

We had arrived at what was now, without a doubt, the legendary secret prison that haunted the secret hearts of Rwandans. The place was the subject of so many rumors and old wives' tales that it was hard to distinguish fact from myth. The locals called it *Akabindi*, after a type of vase with a narrow opening. If something is lost in such a vase, it cannot be lifted out again…

This was the infamous place into which undesirables had, according to rumor, disappeared since the end of the war, never to return.

We walked past windows protected by iron bars. I thought that I could see human faces behind some of them. There was an odor of urine everywhere.

"Remove your shoes and belt."

I obeyed.

"Now your watch, and your wallet."

There stood a pair of junior soldiers nearby, barely teenagers, whom the officer ordered to count my money before taking away the rest of my few belongings.

Another soldier was instructed to open a heavy door and bring me inside. I was quaking with fever, and too weak to offer any argument. They had broken me. I was pointed towards the door, and forcefully pushed through.

This cannot last. There is a mistake. Somehow Jeanne must learn where I am…she can inform the FPR…Afande Kayonga…I will be released soon. Just have to last until then…

I was inside a secure, crowded hall. The air was thick, stuffy, and foul-smelling. I sat down on the concrete floor and tried to breathe deeply and ease my pain. I could hear everything; every sound was amplified and echoed over iron and stone. Guards beating prisoners; prisoners jostling and fighting.

I found myself calling upon my God silently, as I had so many times before. It was nothing like the first night of the genocide, a year before, when I had prayed, with some guilt and hesitation, to a heavenly Father whom I had sorely neglected. I was a very different man now; and I was well aware of His presence with me even before my prayer began.

If you are with me in this place…I need to know, Lord. I am ready to die. But I don't want to.

I still hoped to be released soon, certain that a horrible mistake of some kind had been made. I thought that I would surely be returned to my family as soon as the misunderstanding was made clear. And it was that very ignorance about the future– that expectation of freedom– that was to sustain me for a long time to come. I did not know that I had entered that morning into a second hell, and would be in this prison, and others, for years to come. Had I known it, I might not have found the will to live on until the end.

I hope and wish to write about these things soon, and to speak freely about many others.

From my hard, cold resting place I heard soldiers and officers joking and casually mocking the inmates. The hours of sickness and torture had brought me to an unusual calm. I listened, hardly breathing, and found myself genuinely feeling sorry for them. They were not the framers of whatever policies allowed men like Gaetan and Deo to go to their deaths. They were doing their duty; following orders. But that corruption had poisoned their natures all the same. They did not know love or sanity, neither did they care to learn. I truly pitied them.

It was the Savior, perhaps, answering my prayers from the night before, that I might not die filled with hate.